D0393200

Other Winner Books you will enjoy:
Sarah and the Magic Twenty-fifth, by Margaret Epp
Sarah and the Pelican, by Margaret Epp
Sarah and the Lost Friendship, by Margaret Epp
Sarah and the Mystery of the Hidden Boy, by Margaret Epp
The Hairy Brown Angel and Other Animal Tails,
    edited by Grace Fox Anderson
Danger on the Alaskan Trail (three stories)
Gopher Hole Treasure Hunt, by Ralph Bartholomew
Daddy, Come Home, by Irene Aiken
Patches, by Edith V. Buck
Battle at the Blue Line, by P. C. Fredricks
The Peanut Butter Hamster and Other Animal Tails,
    edited by Grace Fox Anderson
Ted and the Secret Club, by Bernard Palmer
The Mystery Man of Horseshoe Bend, by Linda Boorman

LEE RODDY is a staff writer and researcher for Schick Sunn Classic Productions, Salt Lake City, Utah and a member of the Writers' Guild of America. He is a co-writer of the book which became a TV series, *The Life and Times of Grizzly Adams,* © 1977. He is also a co-writer on the best-selling book, *The Lincoln Conspiracy,* © 1977. He has written and edited for well-known Christians such as Dr. Bill Bright, president of Campus Crusade; Corrie ten Boom; and Brother Andrew. He has worked in radio and on newspapers as well as in TV and movies.

Born in Illinois and reared on a California ranch, Roddy has known horses as long as he can remember. As a child, he spent a lot of time reading about horses and the Old West. Many of these books profoundly influenced his thinking and values. One of his childhood friends, Bonnie Marconette, also loved horses. She shared many memories and fine details about horses with Roddy for this book.

THE TAMING OF CHEETAH

LEE RODDY

A WINNER BOOK

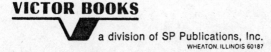

VICTOR BOOKS

a division of SP Publications, Inc.

WHEATON, ILLINOIS 60187

Offices also in Fullerton, California • Whitby, Ontario, Canada • Amersham-on-the-Hill, Bucks, England

All Scripture quotations are from the King James Version.

Second printing, 1980

Library of Congress Catalog Card No. 79-64852

ISBN: 0-88207-486-5

VICTOR BOOKS
A division of SP Publications, Inc.
P.O. Box 1825, Wheaton, IL 60187

Contents

This book is dedicated to
Bonnie Marconette
who loved the original Chita.

CHAPTER 1

A Dream Comes True

SCARCELY able to breathe from fear and excitement, I raised my finger to the auctioneer. "Sixty!" I said it so low he hesitated a moment before nodding.

"Sixty! Sixty!" he took up the chant. "I have sixty. Who'll make it seventy?"

The auctioneer looked toward Ted Dunbar, my lanky, 17-year-old neighbor. He was the only one bidding against me this late spring day. He *would!*

Nervously, I rubbed my work-hardened hands together. I wished my best girlfriend, Arlene Jonsson, was with me. We were both 14 and had just finished our freshman year at high school.

But Arlene was not here, nor was any member of my family. Whatever I did would have to be entirely on my own. I licked my lips and glanced again at the horse which had suddenly entered my life—and might just as suddenly leave it.

The mare was about three or four years old, I figured. Yet she was unbroken—wild as the day she was born.

Obviously, she had never been so close to so many people before. She hadn't stopped running from one end of the arena to the other since she had been let in for the buyers to see.

Experienced ranchers had taken one look at her and decided she wasn't for them. But I had never seen anything so beautiful in all my life. I had to own that mare! So I'd started bidding. Now my heart was pumping like a crazy thing.

I was annoyed when Ted topped my first bid. He didn't need another horse. His dad had a big ranch next to ours, with registered Arabians. But I had spent my life, wanting a horse.

Now that I'd found my dream-come-true, Ted might buy her just to spite me! "Seventy," he boomed across the auction ring. He pushed back his rolled brim cowboy hat, and grinned at me in that teasing way of his.

I was so nervous, my hands trembled as I shoved them into my jeans pockets. I felt the money there. It was all I had. And it had taken me *years* to save that $75. What could Ted know of such scrounging!

"Seventy-five!" I stood up on the lowest fence rail to make sure the auctioneer heard me. He nodded, picked up my bid and began chanting for eighty.

I looked at Ted Dunbar, wondering if he knew that was my last bid—my last dollar.

He squinted at me across the arena and stroked his chin. Would he deliberately outbid me?

"Going once, going twice—" the auctioneer's voice rose above the crowd of curious non-bidders. Ted shrugged. The auctioneer's gavel fell. "Sold to the little girl in the pancake hat!"

I jumped straight into the air with joy. It didn't matter

that the auctioneer had called me a "little girl." The hopes of a lifetime had come true. I had a horse!

"Why'd you want that crazy outlaw?" Ted called as he pushed toward me through the crowd. He wore the faded blue jeans and scuffed boots of a working cowboy. He *did* work hard with his dad, I had to admit that!

"I could ask you the same thing. You don't have a grade mare on your ranch," I said.

"She *is* a beauty!" he remarked, looking at the mare, floating around the corral. Her long black, wavy tail and mane drifted behind her. Her reddish-gold coat glistened with good health. "Wild and beautiful," he added.

"Yes, isn't she?" I said, forgetting my irritation with him for the moment as the mare raced past. She had all the marks of a great horse. The shape of her head was perfect. Her profile was straight from muzzle to forehead. She was wide between her soft brown eyes. Her jowls were wide and tapered down to a delicate muzzle.

"Good conformation," Ted observed. "And look at that unusual bull's-eye of bay hair right in the middle of her forehead."

I grinned as I took in her beauty. She had a white blaze on her face too. Her front legs were unmarked but she had one stocking and one sock on her hind feet. "Her features spell intelligence and a good disposition," I said eagerly. I had my own horse. I was so excited!

"I asked around a little before the bidding began," Ted said. "Nobody seems to know much about her. She could have been born up around Colterville, in gold rush country. You know burros and horses still roam free up there, more like wild deer. Anyway, no matter where she comes from, she's sure to buck when you try to gentle her." His pale blue eyes narrowed with concern.

"She'll do just fine!" I felt my anger coming back as it did so often with him. He didn't need to tell me about my horse!

"Probably be an outlaw," he said, shaking his head soberly. "Maybe even a killer!"

I knew he was half-teasing but I still flared: "You're trying to make me mad because I outbid you!"

"Karen, if I had really wanted her, I wouldn't have let you outbid me," he said. "I couldn't resist needling you to see how high you'd go."

"To my last dollar," I said defiantly. I held up the money. "Every penny I've got. And she's worth it! But, poor thing, she's so scared!"

Ted turned to go. "If you don't break your neck before you decide to sell her, give me a call. I might take her off your hands—for a price." He grinned again, that maddening grin that had so many girls in high school crazy for his attention, but somehow it always just made me *angry*.

"I'll never sell her!" I declared hotly. "Never!"

"Good luck, Karen. You'll need it," he called back.

I made arrangements to have another neighbor, Mr. Kebron, bring the mare home in his trailer. I paid the auctioneer and pedaled back home on my bike as fast as I could. I'd gone to look at a pinto Mom had seen advertised. But he was ugly compared to *my* mare. The tires hardly seemed to touch the ground, I was so happy!

"Mom! Mom! I bought a horse!" I called toward our old frame farmhouse, known around simply as "the Keith Ranch." I skidded to a halt and ran on to the barn and what was left of a bullpen. Years ago, Dad had farmed the place and built two pens, side by side. One pen was long gone, but the other remained. This six-foot high, sturdy corral would certainly hold any horse.

"Did you get the pinto?" Mom asked as she came out of the house. She was a little woman, a head shorter than I. And while my hair was curly and black, hers was brown, going to gray. Her hands were rough and worn from raising my four older brothers and sisters, and me.

"No, he was full of faults," I told her. I hurried around the corral, checking for loose boards and rusty nails. "But wait'll you see the mare I found!"

Mom looked doubtful, as she stood watching me. "I'd heard that the pinto was a good buy," she said.

"Good and ugly," I said, laughing. "But my horse is a beauty!"

"Gentle too?" Mother asked.

I turned toward her a moment. "Well, she's a little scared, Mom."

"I hope you did a wise thing, dear," Mother said. "You know how your father can be sometimes. When he gets back, he might make you get rid of the horse if she doesn't suit him."

"But I paid my own money!" I cried.

"Makes no difference to your father. You know that. I just hope you didn't make a mistake. Someone should have gone along with you."

Mom went back to the house, and I continued to clean out the pen and thought about Dad. He had leased out our ranch land on shares to a bigger rancher and had gone up to the mountains for the summer to work in timber. He didn't like being away from Mom and me, but he needed the good money he'd earn.

We lived along the Stanislaus River, where it enters the great San Joaquin Valley from the Sierra Nevada Mountains, about a two-hour drive from San Francisco.

We were right between two small towns—Riverbend and Oakvalley. We had good land, but our small ranch couldn't compete anymore.

My parents had always worked hard to feed us kids. I guessed that hard work and hard times had helped make Dad kind of stern and stubborn, so I hoped Mom wouldn't phone or write him about the mare. He'd be home in September. I was sure I could gentle her by then.

I was too excited to eat supper. Mom made little clucking sounds but didn't push me. I paced around outside, afterward, waiting for Mr. Kebron. Finally, I heard a vehicle turn off the highway and begin grinding slowly up our long dirt driveway.

It wasn't Mr. Kebron with his trailer, but a stakesided truck that stopped outside our white picket fence. I recognized Ted Dunbar grinning at me from the passenger's side, but didn't know the driver.

Right then I didn't care about him or Ted. My sole interest was the horse standing in the middle of the truck bed. Her feet were spread wide. Her quivering head almost touched the floor. She peered through the racks with wide, anxious eyes and blew her breath out of flared nostrils in quick, noisy snorts. My heart went out to her!

"That crazy mare tore up Kebron's trailer," Ted called, jumping down from the truck cab. "He was so disgusted that he got this man—Mr. Daily—to haul your outlaw."

"She's no outlaw!" I glared at Ted.

Mr. Daily came around the back of the truck. "You know what that horse did?" he asked. "Kebron backed his trailer up to her corral. It took five men to get her in. Then she fought so hard, she wrecked his trailer."

Ted turned to my mother who was approaching. "You should have been there, Mrs. Keith. We managed to get

the mare into the barn, but, man, was she wild! Then Mr. Daily backed the truck up to the barn door."

"Several men got behind her and forced her toward the door," Mr. Daily explained. "When she saw she was cornered—"

"She made a frightened leap right into the truck in an effort to get away from us," Ted finished. "We slammed the tailgate shut and here she is."

"And not too soon for me, either," Mr. Daily said. "I've seen enough of her to last a lifetime. Where do you want her?"

I pointed toward the pen.

Mom shook her head. "Karen, I think you'd better let them take her back—"

"Mom, it'll be all right, really," I interrupted, then ran toward the corral. "She'll calm down, and she'll be just fine!" I called over my shoulder.

The horse didn't move an inch as the truck backed to the open corral gate. She just peered out at me with those big, scared eyes. I soft-talked to her. "It'll be all right. It's all right. Sure."

Ted and the driver lowered the tailgate, which also served as a ramp. The horse rolled her eyes at the opening and suddenly made a flying leap—right into the pen. She never even touched the ramp!

I heard Mom exclaim, "My stars, Karen; what've you done!"

I was too excited to answer. "How much do I owe you, Mr. Daily?" I asked.

"Nothing. It was worth the experience. But I figure Kebron will want something from you for his damaged trailer. Well, so long, Miss."

"See you around," Ted called, climbing into the truck.

"If you decide to sell her—"

"She's not for sale!" I cried.

Ted laughed.

"Karen," Mom said as the truck's growl faded away. "I'm afraid your father will be angry with me."

I hugged her briefly. "No need to tell him for a while. I'll gentle the mare down pretty soon, and she'll be just fine. You'll see. Then you can tell Dad."

"I don't know. I'm afraid you'll get hurt. Such a wild horse!"

I watched with love and excitement as that beautiful, scared animal raced from one end of the pen to the other. Her head was up. She was looking for a way out.

I had a world of respect for her potential to hurt anyone who got too close to her. But her eyes didn't have a mean look—just a look of fear.

"I'm sure all she needs is to learn that I wouldn't hurt her in any way," I told Mom. "But it'll take time for her to realize that."

"I don't know, Karen. I just don't know. She looks untamable to me. If she's three or four years old and nobody has even gentled her a little—"

"Give me some time, Mom. Please!"

Mom turned toward the house. "And be sure you phone Mr. Kebron and find out what we owe him. The good Lord will have to provide the money and look out extra hard for you until your father gets home, Karen. Then don't be surprised if he makes you get rid of her!"

"Aw, Mom, you worry too much!"

She turned to face me. "Karen, the first time you do anything foolish, I'll personally sell her!"

"You can't do that, Mom!" I cried.

"Try me!"

"But you and Dad said I could have a horse!"

"A horse, yes; a wild animal, no! I won't hesitate one minute if it comes to a choice between protecting my daughter and breaking what you consider was my word. And one thing more: If I had to, I'd use the rifle on her, just like I did on that mountain lion when you were a baby!"

Mom walked rapidly into the house. I knew she meant what she had said, but I was too happy about the horse to worry. I walked over and sat down by one of the eucalyptus trees, about 20 feet from the pen. The mare still bolted from one end of the pen to the other.

I figured that eventually she would get so hungry she'd come to the oat hay I'd put in the corner manger. She would gradually overcome her fear of me if I stayed nearby.

I began talking to her in a soft voice. I told her how much I loved and admired her. I teased her because she thought I was such a frightful looking thing that she wouldn't come near me.

She stood alertly in the far corner, outwaiting me. I heard her stomach rumble and growl, but she wouldn't give an inch. And she had to be hungry!

The stars were high and bright when Mom came out and insisted that I come to bed. Reluctantly, I got up and followed her indoors.

Behind me, I heard the mare sigh with relief and trot over to the manger for her meal. Score one for her!

CHAPTER 2

I Name My Horse

I WAS UP with the first rooster's crowing to check on my horse. At the sight of me, she whinnied in alarm and bolted for the far end of the bullpen. She stood there, quivering and blowing. She was so frightened, I ached for her. How I wanted to touch her glossy coat!

"It's all right," I kept telling her. "It's all right. I won't hurt you."

She obviously didn't believe me.

Still, I could wait. And I did! Hour after hour, I spent at the corral, loving that horse and being rejected in return.

The contest went on three days, during which the mare never once made a move toward her feed when I was near. By then, the word had gotten around and people started to show up to see my "wild" horse.

The first one was Mr. Kebron. "Oh-oh," I said to myself when I saw him, "I forgot to phone."

"Well, what're you going to do with that wild animal?" he asked.

"Hope to tame her, Mr. Kebron," I said, then paused.

"I'm sorry I forgot to phone you right away. I hear the mare really tore up your trailer. I guess we owe you something."

He looked down his nose at me for a minute without smiling. "Known you since you were a little tyke, Karen," he said. "You can ferget about the trailer. I'll just knock some new boards on it and it'll be good as new. But we can't knock a few new teeth into your head or new arms and legs on you if you get busted up by that creature. Now, I know your daddy ain't home. I don't think he'd be very happy about you having that horse."

The more he talked, the more nervous I got. "Mr. Kebron, I've wanted a horse of my own all my life. Please don't talk my folks out of letting me have her. Mom said it was OK as long as the mare was no threat."

Our graying neighbor grimaced. Finally he shook his head and walked down the side of the pen to look at the mare. "Guess your ma knows what she's doing. She's raised four pretty smart kids already. But that horse is a wild one!"

I sighed with great relief when he left. I told Mother later that we didn't owe him anything.

"Well, the Lord is looking after us, Karen," she said. "He's given us good neighbors in the Kebrons."

The next visitor was John Riggs. He made a living breaking horses. He was a short, powerful man with shoulders as wide as a barn door. He looked thoughtfully at the mare for a long time. Finally, he asked, "What'd you name her?"

"I'm still debating," I said.

"Maybe just as well you don't name her," he said.

"Why?" I asked.

"It's not so hard to give up something without a name."

"But I'm not going to give her up!" I exclaimed.

"How many horses have you broken, Karen?"

"Well, none yet," I replied.

"You got a good book on the subject, I suppose?" he asked.

"Matter of fact, I do," I answered.

"Would you be interested to know that's the wildest horse I've ever seen in a pen?" he said, nodding toward the mare.

"She's just scared," I protested, tired of the talk.

"And dangerous! Did you know a horse can kill a tiger? I heard about an Indian prince who got mad at one of his horses and put the horse and tiger together in a pen. When the tiger tried to corner the horse, the horse killed him."

I sighed deeply.

"Only way to break that mare is by the whip method," he added.

The thought made me shiver. I'd never known Mr. Riggs to be anything but gentle with horses. Yet here he was, suggesting something mean for *my* horse!

"That way," he continued, "the horse learns to obey the sound of the whip."

"My horse is going to learn to obey through love, not fear," I retorted.

"Sure hate to see you get hurt, Karen," he said. "If you want my honest opinion, I think you're crazy to fool around with that creature."

He left, half-angry. His dust had barely settled in the driveway when the second gloomy "expert" showed up.

Mr. Barstow was a short, thin man with a huge mustache. He'd been breaking and training horses all his life, I knew. He loved animals with a passion. He had a good reputation for working slowly and gently with horses, and he'd had a good training. He walked around the pen, looking the mare over.

Finally he said, "I could break her all right."

"B-but I intend to do it myself," I said, amazed.

He just shook his head like Mr. Kebron and Mr. Riggs. "When you get ready to sell her," he said, as he turned to leave, "give me a call. I might take her off your hands."

By the time he left, I was in no mood to talk to anyone else. So when the next car pulled up, I didn't even turn around.

"God loves you and so does Grandad!" a voice boomed behind me.

I turned around in happy surprise to see Grandad, my mother's father, a big-boned, retired rancher, climbing out of his also-aging car. I ran to meet him. "Oh, Grandad. It's just great to see you!" I cried.

"I even forgive you for not looking around when I come visiting," he kidded me after we'd embraced. Grandad's face was a bit wrinkled, but joy was still bright in his gray eyes.

"Why didn't you write or phone us?" I demanded, taking his scuffed cardboard suitcase. He had often dropped in on us like this when I was younger. He'd stay a week —or several—then go and visit one of his other grown children. Mom was the middle one. But it was at least two years since he'd been at our place.

"What?" he asked in mock horror. "Call ahead and give you a chance to put my picture back on the mantle? No, thanks! I'd rather come unexpectedly and see what you really think of me!"

I laughed. "You're one of my favorite people, and you know it," I said.

"Well, now—" he began. Then he caught sight of the mare. "Say, what've you got there?"

"Come and see!" I said.

"Shouldn't I check in with my daughter and see if I'm welcome?"

I shook my head. "Mom's at the neighbor's. Come on. I want you to see my horse."

We left the suitcase in the dust and walked slowly up to the corral. The mare cocked her ears forward. She arched her neck for a moment, then spun and raced for the far end of the pen.

"Isn't she a beauty, Grandad?" I said, looking up at him.

He stood there, just staring at the mare, then shook his head like all the others. "Never saw a prettier bay. But she's a mite spooky, isn't she?"

"Just scared. She'll be OK," I said.

Grandad walked slowly around the old bullpen, stooping to see through the double, two-by-four boards. The mare watched him fearfully, making those quick, short snorts I'd heard before.

Fear made her brown eyes look twice as large as normal. She was an unforgettable sight.

"What's your father say about her, Karen?" he asked.

"I haven't told him yet."

"I'm not surprised. What about your mother?"

"Oh, she'll be OK."

"Meaning she's about to have a nervous breakdown, huh? Well, can't say I blame her, Karen. That's a mighty wild-looking horse you've got."

"But she's not mean, Grandad," I said. "Look at her eyes."

He cocked his head and ran his hand thoughtfully over

his thinning hair. "Could be you're right, honey," he agreed. "But I wouldn't want anything to happen to you because we misjudged the look in a horse's eyes."

"Aw, Grandad! I thought you'd be on my side!"

"I am, Karen," he replied gently. "I am. That's why I'm sticking my two-bits in without being asked. You got a name for her?"

"Well, I've thought of lots of names—like Storm Cloud or Raindrop. Her coloring suggests things like Copper or Coral. Or Cinnabar."

Grandpa nodded. "She moves nicely too," he said.

I grinned. "Yeah, and she's fast! That's why I've been thinking of calling her Cheetah. Do you like that, Grandad?"

"Sure fits the wild part of her," he said, nodding. "And I hear the cheetah is as fast as the wind."

"And the cheetah's got a sweet, gentle face; not fierce at all," I added. "In fact, cheetahs are sometimes tamed to hunt. We studied about them in school last month." I pushed my hat off my head so it hung by its string around my neck. "Do you think it fits her?" I asked eagerly.

Grandad shrugged, then smiled. "Why not? Guess it'll do her fine."

I hugged him and we went back to the house, picking up his suitcase on the way. I phoned Mom and she came from the neighbor's a short while before Ted Dunbar drove up. I was out in front of the house.

"Give you $50 for the mare," he greeted me.

"That's not funny, Ted," I called back.

"Didn't mean it to be," he said, climbing out of the truck. "I'll give you the money, spot cash." He reached into his jeans' pocket.

"Go away!"

"Look, Karen," he said, seriously, "I'm doing you a favor. No puny girl is going to break that wild horse. It's going to take somebody with a lot of strength."

"Like you, I suppose."

"Like me."

"My horse is not for sale, especially to you."

His grin made me furious. I didn't know what to say because I was so angry. He seemed to sense this, for his grin widened and he walked toward the corral. The mare snorted and spun away. I trailed after him.

"I shouldn't have let you outbid me, Karen," he said. He leaned on a chest-high rail and peered through.

"Don't you have anything to do at home?" I asked.

"I always did like a warm welcome," he said, with a mock sigh. "Well, I can take a hint. Call me when you decide to sell." He walked back to his truck with a tuneless whistle.

I was still fuming when Mom called me for supper. Ted had always irritated me. He was spoiled and self-assured and never asked my opinion. He treated me like a baby, maybe because he was a senior in high school and I was just a "lowly" freshman. Anyway, we just sort of drew sparks, partly, I guess, because I was jealous of the fine horses his dad had.

I washed quickly and sat down at the table. Grandad opposite me bowed his head and prayed when Mom asked him to return thanks.

"Well, Karen," he said afterward, "how're things at church?"

I squirmed a little and kept my eyes on my plate as I ate. "I'm singing in the choir, Grandad," I said.

He smiled knowingly. "Meaning you're still playing church?"

I knew he meant it kindly. But I was still annoyed over Ted's jibes. "Grandad, could we talk about something else?"

"I only asked because I love you, honey," he said. "And there's more to life than horses and choir singing."

I guess Mom sensed tension beginning to build. "Karen's a good girl," she said.

"Nobody knows that better than her grandfather," he said. "But has she accepted Jesus Christ as her Saviour?"

"Look, Grandad," I said, fighting my annoyance, "all my life I've heard about God and Christ and saving souls. I never fight with God or anything like that. But I'm not ready to make any decision right now."

"Karen," Grandad said gently, "I didn't mean to kick over a beehive. I just enjoy being a child of the King so much that I want others to know the joy I have, especially my own granddaughter."

Mom tried again. "Karen's a soloist with the church choir."

Grandad took a bite and chewed thoughtfully. I poked at my food with my fork. I wasn't hungry.

"I'm glad you're singing in the choir, honey," Grandad said, looking up. "Service to the Lord is always good. But I'm still praying for the day when you take the most important step in the world and receive Jesus Christ as your personal Saviour."

"Aw, Grandad, if you're going to keep talking religion, I'm going to leave the table," I said, feeling grumpy.

"Karen!" Mother sounded shocked.

Grandad put up both hands. "Karen, it's just that I love you and God loves you and I'd like you to know Him personally as your mother does."

"But Mom's *old*," I said without thinking. I saw the

hurt look on Mom's face and bit my lip. "I'm sorry, Mom, I didn't mean it that way."

"Honey," Grandad began, "are you saying that 'religion' is for us old folks and not for you? To me, Christianity is just another word for love. Like John 3:16 says, 'For God so loved the world, that He gave His only begotten Son, that whosoever believeth in Him should not perish, but have everlasting life.'"

"I mean it," I said, pushing back my chair.

"All right, dear," Grandad said softly.

We ate in silence then while I fought angry tears.

Finally, Grandad said, "Tell me, what will you do with your horse when she's broken?"

I raised my head, blinking hard. "Ride her all kinds of places. Maybe barrelrace some day. But mostly, she's just for fun."

"What's her background?" he asked.

"Nobody seems to know," I said. "I think she's just horse with a dash of Arabian thrown in. Did you notice her forehead and eyes?"

"Little Morgan in her, I'd guess," he said.

"Could be. Anyway, the important thing is, I love her," I said.

Grandad looked at me in his direct way. "Love is a two-way street, Karen."

"Cheetah will come to love me too," I said.

"Don't get your hopes too high," Mom put in. "I'm going to phone your father long distance Saturday night and tell him about that wild horse. I've got a hunch he'll make you get rid of her right away."

CHAPTER 3

Interfering Neighbor

NO AMOUNT of pleading could make Mom change her mind. I had no choice but to speed up the mare's taming process. That was dangerous, I knew. During the night, I dreamed up an idea that might work.

It had been hard to make a decision with no one to talk to. Like Arlene. She lived across the Stanislaus River, which ran some distance behind our ranch. During the school year, we were inseparable. But as soon as summer vacation started, her folks took off on a trip. Arlene had to go with them. She'd be back soon, but I needed her now.

I had decided to gamble on the mare's training. So I awakened with the first light of dawn. I pulled on my jeans and boots, my older brother's abandoned blue shirt, and my flat, black hat. I hurried out.

Grandad was already up, leaning against the old bull-pen and looking at my horse.

"What are you doing out here so early?" I asked him.

"Occurred to me," Grandad said, "if I was a young girl,

facing a deadline like your mother gave you, I just might do something desperate."

"Such as?"

His eyes crinkled in a smile that caught the dawn light. "Oh, maybe like trying to pen the mare up in the corner by those eucalyptus trees," he said.

I laughed. "Grandad, you've been reading my mind!"

He grinned. "Mighty hard reading the small print. Still, I managed to do that, plus reading the mare's thoughts."

"Her thoughts?"

"Yup. Like what she'll be thinking of doing if somebody tries to nail her into that corner with two by sixes behind her. She'll think she's trapped. And she'll come unglued."

I couldn't help laughing. "Grandad, you should have been born a fox."

"Wouldn't have missed being your grandaddy for anything, Karen. Keeps me struggling to keep up with you."

"Is that a compliment?"

He shrugged. "Don't believe in spoiling my grandchildren. Neither do I believe in letting them get killed."

"Aw, Grandad! Look at her! She's so beautiful! And scared. But she wouldn't deliberately hurt me."

"Not deliberately," he said.

"You don't think my idea will work?"

"Nope. Might start her kicking, and that ruins a horse."

"You got a better idea?" I asked.

"Might have. Make you a trade for it, honey. OK?"

"Sure."

"You stay out of that corral for a while, and I'll try talking your mother out of saying anything to your father just yet."

"Why didn't you say something to her last night?"

He chuckled. "In the nearly 20 years your mother was growing up in my house, I learned one thing about her: Never push when she's got her neck bowed!"

"You think by Saturday night she'll be more relaxed?" I asked.

"It's worth a try. You just stay out of the pen, you hear?"

I nodded. "I'll love Cheetah from afar—for a while."

Grandad helped me move a salt block into the corral. We also fixed the water float on the trough so there would always be fresh water for the mare. She stayed in the far corner, watching us fearfully, every muscle bunched to bolt away.

"Remind me to buy some oats when we're in town," Grandad said. "My gift to Cheetah."

I felt a little better that morning, though I had little reason to be happy. I was uneasy about Mom's deadline, though I knew Grandad probably could persuade her to give me a little more time before telling Dad the mare was unbroken.

A parade of people, coming to offer advice about Cheetah, continued to keep me busy. They all cautioned me, told me I was foolish, then offered to buy her—cheap.

"They all think I'm crazy to try doing anything with her," I told Grandad, "but they sure want to buy her. That last man offered $25!"

The sun was slipping down the western slope of the sky when Cheetah quit racing up and down the corral. She sought shelter from the June sun under the eucalyptus tree. Grandad and I stood in the lengthening shadows on the far side of the pen and looked thoughtfully at her.

"She's got style, Karen," Grandad said. "I watched her with those people. Her action, carriage, head—all good.

No white around the eyes. Everything right to make her a beautiful horse. Smoothest gait I've ever seen too."

"You're falling for her," I said with delight.

"Just checking her over, honey," he said.

We sat in thoughtful silence on the top rail, watching the mare. She had refused to come near the hay I'd held out for her. I compromised, putting it inside the pen near me. The mare looked longingly at it, but wouldn't come near.

"She's real special to you, isn't she, Karen?" Grandad said at length.

I nodded, remembering the hunger of the years—When I was just a little girl, I had started collecting small statues of horses. All kinds. They stood everywhere in my room. And my walls were covered with my own sketches of horses.

"I was just a tiny girl when I first began wanting a pony," I said. "Do you remember, Grandad?"

He grunted, watching the magnificent reddish-gold mare switching flies with her long, black tail. "Sure do. You just about drove your brothers and sisters crazy, not to mention your mom and dad."

"That's what they got for having me 10 years after the other kids," I said with a grin.

Grandad chuckled. "Tell me about when you were a little girl and wanted a pony."

We had plenty of time, so I told him, though he already knew: "Every birthday, every Christmas, it was always the same," I began. "Each Christmas my excitement and hopes built until I was nearly ready to explode. They didn't fade till I had dashed out to look in the horse barn to see if a pony or horse was there.

"I always did it when I thought my folks weren't looking, because I understood in a vague way that they were terribly poor."

Grandad sighed. "Your folks tried to spare you too big a disappointment each year by telling you they couldn't possibly afford to buy or feed a horse for you, Karen."

"I know. But I never completely lost hope. Each Christmas I put new hope in the good Lord, and in Santa Claus. Santa mostly when I was very small. After that it was the Lord's turn."

I glanced at Grandad to see if he was going to take offense at my mentioning the Lord and Santa in the same way, but he seemed to understand what I meant. He just grunted, his eyes on the mare.

"I don't remember ever resenting the fact that my folks never managed to get that pony or horse for me. Somehow, I knew that if they could have, they would have given me one."

Grandad sighed again, as I went on: "I didn't resent Santa Claus or the Lord. I just figured there weren't enough ponies to go around. I was too far down the list, or something like that."

Grandad nodded. "Did you cry?"

"I can't remember. I suppose I did. I do remember that I couldn't eat my breakfast—and how gentle Mom would be without actually saying anything to me. I always knew she understood. Dad too."

Grandad mused, "They used to tell me about it. They were pretty frustrated and sad because you had to be disappointed year after year."

"I guess they were. Anyway, I went through the same soaring hopes and the same heartache afterward whenever my birthday rolled around."

"You had Kate," he said.

"Old Kate! Yes, we had her for years. I lavished a lot of love and affection on that poor old nag. But a workhorse isn't the same as your very own pony."

I laughed now, remembering Dad's plowhorse. "Her lower lip hung down below her upper lip at least an inch," I said. "Her back curved like a rocking chair rocker. But she was a gentle old thing."

"I don't remember horses as well as you, Karen." Grandad smiled. Then he straightened, stretched, and got down off the fence.

I followed him. "Maybe you see why I love this mare so. I've got to gentle her. I've *got* to."

Grandad patted my shoulder. "Patience, honey."

We were almost back at the house when a pickup truck turned off the highway. It was Ted Dunbar.

"Not again," I said, groaning.

"What's the matter?" Grandad asked.

"Oh, it's that pest again."

Grandad squinted at the approaching truck until he made out the circled insignia of the Arabian Horse Association on the panel. "You don't seem very happy, Karen," Grandad said, half-teasing.

"He gives me a pain!"

Ted skidded the pickup to a stop, raising dust. "Hi! You still trying to figure out how to train that wild animal?"

"I'm working on it," I said with as much politeness as I could spare.

"Well, if you'd like some help—"

"I don't need your help! Go away. Come on, Grandad, let's go inside."

Grandad frowned. "My granddaughter doesn't mean to be rude, young man."

"Grandad! Don't apologize for me!"

"We've been fighting for years," Ted said cheerfully. He was so exasperating sometimes! "I'm Ted Dunbar," he said, sticking out his right hand. "Guess you're Karen's grandfather?"

"Ed Martin," Grandad said, shaking hands. "You a Christian, Ted?"

Ted got a funny look on his face.

I nearly died. "Grandad!"

"No offense," Grandad said to Ted, "but I always like to know if people I meet have accepted Christ."

"I've never had much to do with religion, if that's what you mean," Ted replied, cautiously.

"Like to talk to you about it sometime, Ted," Grandad went on. "You see, I'm one of those Christians who enjoys his religion, and—"

I tugged at his arm. "Grandad!"

He yielded, walking with me. "I was just practicing the 107th Psalm, honey: 'Let the redeemed of the Lord say so.' Why're you so upset?"

"You embarrassed me to death!" I whispered fiercely as we approached the house.

"Why?" he asked. "Because I care enough to ask about the boy's salvation?" he said.

"People don't go around asking questions like that!" I replied.

"That's their problem," Grandad said calmly. "You think I'm blunt as a warclub, don't you? Well, I'm old enough to have learned a few things about the world.

"One is that you never catch fish if you don't make connections. Another is that I don't want to someday face my Maker and have Him say that I didn't speak to someone about Christ when I had a chance."

"Grandad, I understand how you feel. But you just can't do things like you just did!"

"You defending the boy?" he asked.

"Ted? Certainly not! I wouldn't care if he never showed his face again. But, well, I guess I'm thinking of myself." I lowered my eyes, suddenly ashamed.

Grandad seemed to read my thoughts. He quoted Paul: " 'For I am not ashamed of the Gospel—' " He turned toward the horse corral and broke off suddenly.

I spun around, alarmed.

The fence was two by fours bolted together and staggered, one board in, the next out, at the posts. This made a stronger pen. It also made it harder to see through, and posed a danger I hadn't thought of until the moment it happened.

Ted Dunbar stood in the middle of the corral. He was swinging a lariat around his head. The mare had backed into the far corner, watching with terror the boy and his rope.

"Ted! No!" I screamed and ran toward the corral.

The rope hissed out, aimed for the pointed ears. Instantly, Cheetah jumped aside. The rope hit her shoulders. She snorted in fright, danced uncertainly, then ran straight at Ted.

He yelled, waved his arms at her, then grabbed for the fence.

Cheetah swapped ends, neighing in terror. She ran for the far fence. She did not slow up.

"No! Cheetah, no! You can't jump that—" My words were wasted.

Gathering all her muscles into a knot, the mare launched herself for the top rail.

Most horses can't jump high. Only Cheetah's front fore-

feet went over the top board. Her chest hit the fence with a terrible sound. Instantly, the mare fell.

For one terrible moment, her front hooves scraped down the two by fours. Then I saw the right hoof safely touch the corral dust. The left hoof caught on the second board from the bottom—an outside board.

I still ran, too frightened to cry out.

But I knew that if that forefoot slipped down behind the bottom board, pinning the slim leg between the inside and outside rails, only one thing could happen: The leg would break and the mare would have to be shot!

CHAPTER 4

A Hog and a Stallion

I BARELY noticed Ted clinging to the fence as I grabbed the top rail and scrambled over. I landed inside the corral directly in back of the fallen mare. I saw her terror-stricken eyes leave Ted and rest on me.

"Easy, Cheetah! Easy!" I spoke quietly, forcing myself to stand still. I didn't want to frighten her any more. My eyes focused on the endangered leg while my mind whirled.

Cheetah's nostrils flared. Her magnificent reddish-gold body rested in the dust as though the wind had been knocked out of her.

"Be careful!" Ted yelled. "She tried to run me down!"

"She was just trying to get past you," Grandad said through the fence. "Karen, you watching her leg?"

"Yes, Grandad! If it slips between those boards—"

"I know. Honey, walk away from her, but stay where she can see you. Keep walking until I tell you, then move slowly toward her!"

"But—"

36

"Hurry! She's getting back her wind!"

I obeyed him. If she moved away from me when I approached, she probably would pull the endangered leg quickly and safely back.

"Now!" Grandad's voice was strong but quiet.

I changed directions, moving on an angle toward the mare's outstretched foreleg. "Lord, please! Don't let her break a leg!"

Cheetah's wide eyes clung to me. I spoke softly to her. Carefully, slowly, I moved toward her. I saw her glistening hide ripple as she gathered her muscles.

With a sudden snort and toss of her head, Cheetah started to get up. She put her weight on the right hoof. Almost in the same movement, she drew the endangered left foreleg back and under her. Then she was up!

With a quick neigh, she whirled and thundered away to the far end of the corral.

I sighed with relief.

"Good thing a horse always gets up front-end first, instead of like a cow," Grandad said. "She had to have both legs to support her weight."

I didn't say anything. I was shaking so badly.

Then I remembered Ted Dunbar. I spun around and headed toward him.

"Now, wait a minute!" he said as he scrambled over the fence. "I was just trying to help!"

"I don't want your help!" I yelled. "I didn't ask for it! When I get my hands on you, Ted Dunbar—"

"Hold on, honey!" Grandad's firm command slowed me. He glanced at the boy. "Maybe you'd better head on home, young fellow."

Ted muttered something and wordlessly headed for his pickup. Still shaking, I watched him, until he started the motor. He stuck his head out the window and yelled, "She's crazy! Absolutely crazy! She'll kill somebody. Wait and see!"

When the dust of his pickup began to settle, I climbed over the fence and stood beside Grandad. "Do—do you think he's right, Grandad?"

He put his arm around my shoulder. "Honey, he just scared that poor mare silly. But I don't think she's crazy. Look at her!"

Cheetah stood, tense and trembling, at the far end of the corral. I ached to reassure her, to make her know she was loved and wanted and nothing was going to hurt her. I began talking to her, soothing her. That's when I saw the blood.

"Grandad, look!"

"I saw it. Streak of blood on her chest where she hit the fence. But I don't think it's too serious. And even if it is, she's not going to stand still so you can help her."

"Oh, you poor, beautiful thing!" I said to her. "Oh, Cheetah, Cheetah!"

"Better just make sure she has hay and oats in the manger," Grandad suggested. "Then let's back off and let her calm down." He turned thoughtfully to look toward the sun. "Matter of fact, probably the best thing we could do right now would be to go fishing."

"You're joking!"

"Never more serious. Come on, I'll get the tackle."

I didn't want to go, but Grandad insisted. I helped him find the shovel and dig some worms, but my eyes kept straying to the mare. Even in her fright, she was beautiful!

She was searching for a way out of the pen, trotting back and forth from one end to the other, her head high.

"She's just working off steam," Grandad said. "Come on. I've got the urge to catch a nice mess of fish."

We walked past the unused cow barn with pigeons and sparrows calling from the high rafters inside. We turned down the lane the cows had once used, cut across the pasture, now rented out, and moved through the almond orchard.

Ranching hadn't brought in a lot of money for Dad, but it had been a living. My parents had made enough off their Grade-B dairy and the crops to raise a family. However, the price-cost squeeze in recent years had forced Dad out of ranching, along with a lot of other people. My two older brothers and two older sisters had left the ranch to live in the city. They had children of their own and didn't often come to visit.

"Guess this will all be subdivision in a few years," Grandad said. "Shame too. But it seems everybody in the city wants to live in the country, even if they have to turn the country into a city to do it."

I nodded. "Dad's just hanging on to the land, figuring to eventually subdivide. Everything's moving this way, just as you said."

Grandad came to the barbed wire and hog wire fence that separated the back of our place from Dunbar's property. The mares and foals allowed to roam here were wire-wise. They didn't try to go through the fence.

"Sure peaceful out here," Grandad mused. He put one heavy shoe on top of the hog wire and held up the bottom of the three barbed-wire strands. "Can you slide through there without ripping your britches?" he asked.

"I've done this hundreds of times," I said as I slipped neatly through, then held it for him. "In fact," I told him, "Arlene and I went through here so often we got to be like coyotes, jumping through without touching a hair."

Grandad's eyes sparkled with amusement. "Sure hope you two didn't catch all the fish out of the river since I was here last." We walked toward the line of cottonwoods.

"We don't come down here often anymore," I said.

"Why? Too grown-up, or is the fishing bad?"

"We never fished much. We climbed the wild grapevines that grew up through the trees along the river bottom. And then, there were the wild hogs."

"Oh, yes. The hogs. I'd almost forgotten them." Grandad frowned.

"Keep a sharp eye out for them," I said. "They don't often come this far, but you never know."

We moved on toward the river, not talking. It was wonderfully peaceful. A redheaded woodpecker drilled on a dead river oak, his feet and tail holding him up on the side of the tree. A yellowhammer flew by in long, undulating glides. Somewhere in the dense trees ahead a bird I'd never been able to identify called out in a series of quivering notes. And the smell of the river and trees—mostly cottonwood, with some willows and oaks—was in the air.

Grandad led the way down the narrow path through the yellow, waist-high weeds. A row of wild blackberry vines, high as a garage, grew along a shallow ravine that fed the river in the springtime. Twisted wild grapevines hung invitingly from the trees.

It was truly peaceful. For a while, I even forgot Cheetah.

A jackrabbit leaped up in front of Grandad, and my heart leaped too. "Thought it was a wild hog," I told Grandad. The rabbit ran straight ahead on the trail. His tall, black-tipped ears stuck straight up. His long hind legs propelled him ahead in smooth flight.

"Glad there's still some wildlife around," Grandad said over his shoulder. "That's the first animal I've seen down here. A few years ago, it was full of game. Too many people around now, I guess."

Grandad paused a moment, squinting ahead at the river. He pointed his cane pole. "Looks like a pretty good spot," he said.

"Not over there, Grandad."

"Why not?"

"That's where Arlene and I have seen the wild hogs."

"Well, we sure don't want to tangle with them, do we? Which way's safe?"

I pointed down the river. "We usually go that way."

Grandad nodded and turned the way I'd indicated.

Years ago, even before Dunbars bought the property, some pigs had gotten loose from their pen. Ever since, they'd roamed down in the river bottom, foraging off the land. The pigs had grown into huge, ugly hogs. Their descendants had become wilder and bigger. I was deathly afraid of them.

"Look out!" Grandad stopped suddenly as the ground seemed to explode under him. He jumped back, almost knocking me down. I dropped my pole, trying to keep my balance.

The river grass parted and a huge black boar stood there. His wicked tusks curled up past an ugly, bluish snout. The scarred leathery ears dropped past mean little eyes.

"Stay still!" Grandad's voice was surprisingly calm.

Goosebumps chased themselves up and down my arms, and my hair felt as if it were sticking straight up.

The boar was about 15 feet away. He must have weighed 300 pounds.

For a long moment, he just stared and we stared back.

Then, off to our right, the grass began exploding like popcorn. Half a dozen smaller hogs—red, black, speckled, and mixed—scooted off in all directions. Fortunately, they ran away from us, squealing in fright.

With a single gruff grunt, the huge boar turned and followed them at a dead run.

"Whew!" I breathed at last. "That was close!"

Grandad looked a little pale. He took off his hat, rubbed the back of his hand along his forehead, and sat down on the path.

I did the same.

"I remember, years ago, seeing a friend of mine swing his leg over a pigpen," Grandad said. "There was a boar in that pen about the size of the ugly brute we just saw."

Grandpa paused, looking in the direction the wild hogs had gone.

"What happened?"

"You'd never guess so big an animal could move so fast. That hog dashed across the pen before my friend could get his leg out of the way. The boar's tusks went right through my friend's boot and leg like a hot knife through butter. If there hadn't been several of us there to help him, my friend might have been finished right then."

I shuddered. "I've never heard of anybody actually getting hurt by these wild hogs, but I'm really scared of them. A minute ago, I thought we were goners."

Grandpa smiled weakly. "Can't say I blame that old fellow for jumping up, mean-looking and ready to fight. It was my fault. I almost stepped on his hind pocket. Must've disturbed his sleep!"

We both chuckled. "No more quiet walking to enjoy listening to nature," I assured him. "From now on, I sing while I walk. Even if it scares the fish away."

Grandad stood up. "Good Lord takes care of His own, Karen. Come on. First one to catch a fish doesn't have to clean any."

We went noisily on to the river and began to fish.

We spent a pleasant hour or two. The river wasn't as wide as it used to be, nor as clean. But this particular section was fenced off a couple of miles upstream. Not many people poked through this area, especially those who knew about the wild hogs.

"Seems to me," Grandad said after we'd sat quietly for a while, "if I were you, I'd pull in my line."

I glanced at my cork. It was moving rapidly out into midstream, underwater. I gave a mighty yank. The tip of the pole flew up, followed by the line, cork, sinker—and empty hook. The sinker wrapped the hook and line around an overhead limb.

Grandad laughed heartily. "You fishing for birds, honey? I always found fishing was better in the water."

I tugged uselessly at the snarled line. "I'll still catch the first fish, and you'll have to clean both yours and mine," I teased back.

I gave up trying to retrieve my line. I cut it and began to rig up a new hook and sinker. Just then Grandad tensed as his cork began to move.

"What was that you said about catching the first fish?" he asked quietly. He waited until the cork vanished, then gave a slight jerk on the pole. The tip bent and the line sliced through the water.

A sudden drumming of hooves behind us made us both swivel around.

A chocolate-red stallion swept by, neighing a challenge to the world. Gold highlights glittered on his glossy hide. His powerful neck, arched proudly, was graced with flying mane. He was a perfect picture of wild strength and beauty.

"What was that?" Grandad asked in awe as the stallion disappeared through the trees.

"Dunbar's stallion, Sinbad. He's a champion Arabian."

"Magnificent!" Grandad almost breathed the word.

"You lost your fish," I told him.

"It was worth it. I haven't seen a horse like that in years. Does he often go racing through here?"

"Ted and his father usually keep him penned up near their house. Guess he's just out for a run today."

"Well, he certainly was feeling his oats. What a sight!" Grandad stared after the horse. I knew how he felt.

"Stallions can be dangerous, you know," Grandad warned. "You'd better remember that. Always stay away from him. And keep your mare away too."

"Aw, Grandad! I'm not afraid of Sinbad! Why, I remember the first time I rode him. He's no trouble."

"Just the same, you remember what I said. And keep your mare penned well. If she ever got loose down here, you'd never get her away from him."

"Wonder what kind of a colt they'd have?" I mused.

"Better forget about horses and tend to fishing," Grandad said. "Otherwise, you're likely to lose that pole of yours in the river."

I pulled out my first fish, forgetting then what Grandad had said about the stallion. But I would remember later.

CHAPTER 5

Reprieve

SATURDAY MORNING found me feeling uneasy. I dressed early and went to feed Cheetah. She still ran from me. All the time I talked to her and worked around, filling her manger with oats and hay, she stayed at the far end of the corral. It was discouraging, to say the least. And tonight—

Grandad eased my mind on that score when he came to call me for breakfast.

"You look like the cat that swallowed the canary," I said to him.

He squinted through the corral at Cheetah. "All us cats grin like that on Saturday morning."

My hopes began to rise. "You talked to Mom?"

He grinned at me. "She's not going to tell your father about the mare when she phones him tonight."

I threw my arms around Grandad's waist and laid my head on his chest. "Grandad, you're the greatest!"

He teased, "I always knew that, and your mother knew it, but I wasn't sure about you."

"How'd you do it?" I asked, looking up at his sparkling eyes.

"Trade secret," he said, winking broadly. He shifted his eyes to Cheetah. "How's she doing?"

I sighed. "No change."

Grandad snorted so loudly he made Cheetah jump. "No change, my foot! She's wilder than before!"

I walked toward the gate. Grandad followed. "It's Ted's fault," I said. "He scared her with that lasso."

"Well, it can't be helped now. At least you have a reprieve from your mother. But I stuck my neck out for you, Karen, so you've got to be extra careful with that horse. You got a plan?"

I stepped up on the gate boards and peered over at the mare. "Just to outlove her."

"That's the best way, of course. But it may take all summer, or longer. Your father will be home September first."

"Do you suppose I can be riding her by then?"

"Not much chance, I'd guess. Fact is, if you even get to touch her by then, I'll be surprised."

I looked at Grandad in dismay. "You're kidding!"

He shook his head. "You'll need a stack of patience."

"Well," I said, watching the alert ears swivel toward me with each word, "she's worth it."

"You just going to sit here, hour after hour, talking to her?"

"Except when Mom makes me clean up my room or help with the dishes and housework. Seven days a week."

"Not tomorrow, I hope."

"Sure. Why not?"

"It's the Lord's Day."

"Well, it won't hurt if I miss church now and then.

I hate to break the pattern of coming here each day."

"Bible says even animals get the Sabbath off."

I laughed and put my arm around Grandad's waist. "Who can argue with logic like that?"

"Glad you see it the right way," he said. "Come on. Time for breakfast."

The rest of the day went easy enough. Mom made me clean my room, but I zipped through that and returned to the corral. The oats and hay were gone. That posed another problem: I'd soon have to start buying my own feed. Which meant I'd need a job that would take me away from the mare.

Well, I'd cross that bridge when I came to it.

After supper that night, Grandad leaned back in his chair. "Tell your mother about the stallion we saw on the river."

Mom stopped knitting the afghan she was working on. "The chocolate-colored one?"

"Sinbad sailed by while Grandad and I were fishing."

"I'm afraid of that horse," Mom said seriously. "Always have been."

"I'm not afraid of him," I announced. "He's gentle as a doll. You remember when I first rode him, Mom, don't you?"

"Wasn't that the time you met Ted?" she said.

"Right after he and his dad moved here. You see, Grandad," I said, turning to him, "I was out riding Kate, bareback, not going anyplace special, when I saw my dream horse coming down the road. That's the first time I remember seeing Ted. He was riding that Arabian stallion."

"I remember," Mom said, "you rode right up to the window here. And Ted looked so funny—"

"You're getting ahead of the story, Mom," I said.

"Sorry, dear," she said, smiling.

"Well," I continued, "Sinbad came galloping down the road like a ship with all sails flying, as Ted once said. The horse actually glistened in the sunlight."

Grandad smiled. "Sounds like a commercial for something or other."

"He was a dream. He tossed his head and stepped like a dancer. I still remember the arch in his neck."

"The boy's?"

"Oh, Grandad! Of course not! The horse's. Oh, he was pretty. You can imagine how silly I felt sitting bareback on that old plowhorse. But I wasn't going to let that fancy stallion out of my sight. I struck up a conversation with the boy."

"And that's how you got acquainted with Ted Dunbar —the young fellow you fight with now?"

I nodded. "He'd just moved into the area. His father figured on raising Arabians for show. He'd just bought the young stallion to keep for the time when he could afford registered Arabian mares, as he has now."

"How long ago was that?"

"About two years, right after you were here last."

"What happened after you talked the boy into letting you ride the stallion?" Grandad asked.

"It was only half a mile or so to our house from where we met, so I talked Ted into trading horses. He got on Kate and I got on Sinbad and away we went!"

"Any trouble holding the stallion in?" Grandad asked.

"None. He responded perfectly to my commands. I was so excited, though, it was all I could do to keep from letting Sinbad run."

Grandad listened attentively. "Go on."

"Poor Ted! He couldn't convince old Kate that he wanted to keep up with me. Kate stubbornly continued to plod along while Sinbad and I loped down the road."

I paused, but neither Mom nor Grandad said anything. "I looked back once to see Ted kicking vainly at old Kate's sides, trying to make her break out of her usual slow walk. I knew I wasn't being very polite by riding out ahead of him, but I just couldn't wait to show the horse to Mom. I knew Ted couldn't get hurt on Kate, so Sinbad and I just sailed on, into our yard."

Mom added, "She stopped right outside the window there and called me. She was all excited."

"The funny thing," I continued, "was old Kate, plodding in with Ted vainly trying to speed her up. She clopped into the yard, not caring a bit about being left behind. Ted was furious." I laughed, remembering.

"Is that when you and Ted began to tangle?"

"No, Grandad. We got along at first. But Ted was pretty spoiled. He's alone with his dad. His mother died a year or so before they moved here and Ted's father has given him just about anything he wants."

"You ever ride that stallion again?"

"Off and on. But when Mr. Dunbar began to build up his string of brood mares, Sinbad wasn't ridden much."

Grandad cleared his throat. "Stallions can be unpredictable. Sometimes they bite and kick and get pretty mean."

"But others stay as gentle as kittens," I protested.

The conversation drifted off to why horses shy at things. "Most horses seem to shy at pieces of paper," I reminded them. "You ever notice that, Grandad?"

He nodded. "Especially paper rolling and skipping across the road in front of them."

Mom looked up from her knitting. "Kate, as old as she was, used to have fun pretending she was scared half out of her wits when she'd see paper flying around."

Grandad pursed his lips. "Years ago, when I rode a lot, it seemed that whenever I'd settle down a bit tighter into the saddle, I could expect my horse to find something like that to liven things up a little."

Mom looked at me. "I remember a gelding your father had when you were little. When he'd see a piece of paper, he'd throw his head up, flare out his nostrils, and either jolt to a stop by planting all four feet out wide, or stop and stand there quivering and snorting, looking like a keg of dynamite with the fuse lit. Or sometimes that horse would give a couple of snorts and try to bolt for the barn."

I remembered that white cement bridges and supports usually brought on the same nervous behavior, though to a lesser degree.

Mom stood up. "You two can sit here telling horse stories all night, if you want to. But it's time for me to place that long distance call to your father."

I glanced at Grandad, and he winked.

"He'll want to talk to both of you," Mom said. She spoke to Dad first and hinted that I had something to tell him. Then she handed the phone to me.

I held my breath for fear Dad would ask about the mare's disposition and I'd have to say she was sort of wild. I couldn't lie to him.

Right away he said, "I hear you have news for me."

"I got a horse, Daddy. A four-year-old mare. She's so beautiful. Wait'll you see her!"

"I'm glad, Karen." The hum on the farmers' line made Dad's voice seem very far away. "A good buy then?"

"Oh, yes, Daddy."

"Keep her away from barbed wire."

"I will. Here's Grandad. He wants to talk to you."

I handed the receiver over and took a deep breath. Well, one hurdle passed. I still had some time to tame Cheetah. I went to the corral after family devotions to check on her.

She ran, snorting, to the far end of the pen. There she stood, every muscle quivering in the weak light of the outside reflectors on the abandoned tankhouse and barn.

I kidded her about being such a scaredy cat. "You don't have to be afraid of me," I reminded her. "I wouldn't hurt you. I love you."

Cheetah snorted noisily.

Oh, well, I had most of the summer to win her.

I glanced at the sky. It was black above the eucalyptus trees. Jillions of stars twinkled at me. Crickets sang a spring chorus in the grass by the barn and deep-voiced bullfrogs took up solo parts. A slight breeze ruffled the topmost leaves of the trees.

It was like being in church. There was something in Psalms—A faint squeak broke my thoughts. I glanced around but saw nothing unusual. Cheetah didn't seem disturbed.

I took a deep breath. Time for bed. I started back toward the house. My eyes took in the lights at Ted Dunbar's. I wondered if he was thinking about how he was going to get Cheetah. Well, let him try!

I stopped, hearing the squeak again. What was it? I turned back toward the corral, listening and wondering.

It came again. This time I saw it.

Slowly, very slowly, the corral gate began to swing open—by itself.

CHAPTER 6

Arlene Comes Home to Tragedy

I STARED HARD at the gate. A vagrant wind had dropped from the treetops to the ground. The evenly balanced gate, pushed by that gentle breeze, was opening outward.

I realized the danger and sprinted for the gate. But Cheetah had seen the opportunity for escape. She neighed and bolted for the opening. Naturally she outran me, but I had another advantage. I raised my arms and let out a yell that scared even me.

Cheetah drew up sharply, sliding back on her hindquarters and raising a lot of dust. She twisted around, whinnied, and raced to the far end of the corral.

I reached the gate, shoved it closed, and slammed the wooden slide bolt. I shuddered to think what would have happened if I hadn't been there.

"Karen! What's the matter?" Mom called from the house. She and Grandad came running from the back door. The outside lights were on so their shadows bounced crazily along as they ran.

"The gate was open! It's all right. I got here just as Cheetah dashed for freedom."

"My stars! How did the gate get opened?" Mother asked.

"I don't know," I said, examining the bolt.

Grandad and Mom reached me, puffing a little. Mom said, "You must have left the slide out, Karen."

"I'd never be that careless."

"Don't look at me!" Grandad said, breathing hard.

"Needless to say," Mom added, "I haven't been around the corral all day."

"Somebody had to leave the gate unbarred," I said a little angrily. "I certainly didn't do it."

Mom was catching her breath. "You must be mistaken, dear."

"But I'm positive I didn't leave that gate unlatched," I said.

"Then how was it opened?" Mom asked.

I had an angry thought. "Was Ted Dunbar here today?"

Mom and Grandad agreed he had not been.

"There's only one answer, then," Grandad said. He walked to the gate and felt the inside pin on the slide bolt.

"What's that?" I asked, watching him curiously.

"Cheetah opened the gate herself."

"Aw, Grandad!"

"Some horses can open gates. Especially easy ones like this, with a smooth-working slide bolt and properly hung hinges."

"Even if a horse could get hold of the handle, how could he pull the bar back six inches and free the latch?"

"With teeth. Here. Feel the inside handle. Might be teeth marks I'm feeling."

I felt the slide bar handle. It was simply a dowel run through a hole in the wooden slide bar. The pin was used to pull the bar in and out of the square hole in the fence post. "I don't feel anything," I said.

"Maybe just my imagination," Grandad confessed. "I knew of a gelding that could open gates. He had a knack for it. He'd just take the pin in his teeth and move his head sideways. Presto! Open gate!"

"I don't believe Cheetah opened this gate."

"Then how do you figure it happened?" Mom asked.

"I'll bet Ted Dunbar had something to do with it."

"Now, Karen, that's not likely," Mom chided.

Grandad grunted. "I think you're barking up the wrong tree there, Karen. But no matter what you think, you'd better put a stronger latch on this gate. If the mare escapes, you'll have real troubles."

"OK," I agreed, "I'll fix it. But I still don't see how Cheetah could work that bolt loose by herself."

I went to the tankhouse, found some old baling wire and fashioned a double twisted loop. I took it to the gate and forced it down over the gate post and the solid post into which the bolt slid. "There," I said to Cheetah where she stood snorting at the far end of the corral, "that should hold you."

Grandad's voice roused me the next morning. I opened my eyes to full daylight. It was the first morning I hadn't awakened around dawn. I jumped up and ran to the window.

"She's all right," Grandad said, chuckling. "But since you were such a sleepyhead, I've already fed your horse."

"I dreamed all night," I confessed. "Terrible dreams about Cheetah getting out and running away."

"Well, since it was only a dream, it seems you've got an

extra reason to get to church. In fact," he said with a grin, "it seems to me that since your prayers of a lifetime have been answered, you'd be extra anxious to show the good Lord some gratitude."

"I already thanked Him. But not in church," I said.

I sat down on the corner of the bed and contemplated my bare feet. After years and years of praying, I *did* finally have my answer. "But I'm not so sure prayer really had anything to do with it," I said aloud.

"How's that?" Grandad asked from the doorway.

"I prayed for 10 or 12 years and absolutely nothing happened until I was big enough to earn my own money to buy a horse."

"You want me to tell the Lord that for you while you sleep in?" Grandad asked.

"Oh, Grandad!" I threw my pillow at him.

He grinned happily and closed the door so I could dress. I hated to wear a dress, but Mom hated to have me go in the jeans I wore all week. She always claimed that if she had wanted another boy, she'd have had one. But she wanted a girl, and I was that girl and someday maybe I'd grow out of the tomboy stage and quit wearing jeans everywhere except to church. Mom liked Sundays, she said, because it gave people a chance to see she had a daughter.

Arlene went through the same thing with her parents, but to a lesser extent. Arlene wore dresses around the house sometimes. I wondered how soon they'd be home from their trip, and how her gelding, Nipper, was getting along. Usually, I'd have been over feeding and riding him, although the Jonsson's had a man who took care of the place when they were away. Still, I had a momentary sense of guilt for neglecting Nipper because of Cheetah.

We started for church all right, but never made it.

We were riding toward town with Mom at the wheel when Grandad leaned forward. He looked strange in his old, out-of-style suit and dress shoes. He pointed through the windshield. "Something's going on up there."

I looked. "It's a girl running along the roadway. And what's she got in her hand?"

The car rapidly overtook the girl. Mom and I both said it at once. "Arlene Jonsson!" And she was carrying a halter. We pulled up alongside her, and I opened the back car door.

"Arlene! What's wrong?"

"Oh, Karen! Nipper got out! He's just ahead, around that curve." She climbed into the car and plopped down beside me. She wore dirty blue jeans and a short-sleeved boy's shirt. Her short brown hair, cut like mine, was uncombed. Her deeply tanned face was smudged with dirt. She was obviously scared silly.

"We'll give you a hand," I told her. "When did you get back?"

Mom eased the car forward. Arlene rubbed her forehead. I caught a whiff of the good fragrance of the real leather bridle she was holding.

"Mom got sick and we had to come back early," she explained, peering ahead between Mom's and Grandad's shoulders. "Oh, nothing serious. In fact, Dad says Mom just got homesick and made herself just sick enough physically that we had to come home."

"Arlene, guess what?" I said, feeling my happiness well up inside. "I got a horse!"

"You did? Oh! Oh! There he is!"

We rounded the corner. Nipper was trotting along the road shoulder, head high, watching some cows through a barbed wire fence. He caught sight of our car and broke into a lope.

"Good thing you came along," Arlene said, "or I'd never have caught him."

"You haven't caught him yet," Grandad reminded her.

"Oh, he'll be all right when he gets the kinks out of his legs," Arlene explained. "He's just been cooped up too long. The gate was left open, and he took off."

"Your gate was left open too?" I asked.

"Well, I don't know whether it was left open or somebody opened it or what, but I do know Nipper got out and he's liable to get killed."

We pulled up slowly behind the gelding. He was a nice sorrel; nothing fancy, but a good riding horse and usually as mild-mannered as a puppy. Only today he was feeling frisky, running down the public road.

"Oh! Oh! Stop!" Arlene surprised Mom, and she hit the brakes hard. My seatbelt bent me sharply forward. Arlene, without a belt, almost cracked her head on the back of the front seat. She recovered quickly, opened the door and jumped out on the roadway the moment we stopped.

Nipper had stopped at the fence to whinny at a horse in a pasture beyond the one with the cows. He turned to look at Arlene as she approached, one hand out in front of her as though she had feed in it; the one with the halter was behind her back.

"Easy, Nipper! Easy!" Arlene said. The gelding watched her uncertainly.

I wondered if I should get out and help her or if I'd start him running again. I decided to sit still since Arlene was almost within reach of Nipper.

Just then a car rounded the curve behind us, shot past

at a high speed, and blasted his horn, as he hurtled on toward town.

Startled, Nipper started running again. This time he ran back the way we'd come. Arlene jumped back in the car. "Would you mind turning around and going after him?" she asked. "A car could hit him."

Mom turned the car around and we caught up with Nipper again. We were all angry with the driver who'd honked. In this state, horses had the right of way over vehicles. Of course, most people didn't know that. And many drivers didn't realize how dangerous it could be to honk at a horse.

"He's tiring," Arlene said as we pulled up behind Nipper. "I'll get him this time."

She would have too, except that another car came along behind us, passed fast, and a piece of paper fluttered out the window. "Litterbugs!" I muttered angrily.

Nipper saw the paper, shied violently away from it, and ran right into the barbed wire fence. Instinctively, he kicked at the thing which punctured his skin. He caught his hind foot and fell sideways on the fence.

"Oh, no!" It could have been Arlene's cry—or Mom's. Nipper went down, breaking off a fence post. In his struggle to get back up, he became entangled in the sharp strands of wire, like an insect caught in a web.

We all jumped out of the car and ran toward him. Nipper struggled frantically, making the mess worse. He was tearing his hide and blood showed in various places. His terrified whinnies pierced the air and tore at my heart. The wire creaked and snapped but it held.

All of us were calling to Nipper, trying to calm him. But nothing worked. Nothing reached through his fear.

"He's bleeding! He's bleeding awful bad!" Arlene cried,

holding her shaking hands just inches off her pasty face. "Oh, Nipper! Nipper! Hold still!"

"You got a pair of wire cutters in the car?" Grandad asked Mom.

She shook her head. "Everything's in the pickup that Tom drives. I can't fix anything, so I never carry tools."

Grandad grunted. He took off his Sunday coat and threw it in the car. His tie fluttered in the spring air as he hurried toward the fallen horse. All of us moved in, but not too close. Nipper was kicking crazily with his two free legs.

"He'll weaken in a minute," Grandad said. Then he glanced at Arlene and changed his wording. "He'll settle down in a minute. I'll try to get him free while you girls hold his head. Go around him but keep away from his hooves!"

Gradually, Nipper's wild struggles quieted down. Arlene and I came to his head, talking calmly. Grandad struggled with the wire, but each time he tried to free a section, it tore into Nipper and caused him to start struggling again.

I glanced at Arlene's face. She was pasty white and tears made streaks through the dirt on her face. I ached for her, my best friend. Yet deep inside I was glad it was her horse instead of mine that lay bleeding in a tangle of barbed wire.

I looked back at Grandad. You wouldn't think there was so much blood in all the world.

"If we can get a tourniquet on that hind leg," Grandad said, puffing a little with his efforts, "maybe we can stop the worst bleeding."

"How about my belt?" I asked, whipping it off.

Grandad grabbed it without even taking his eyes off

the horse. "Better see if you can stop the worst of those other cuts," he said.

Mom stopped at a gopher mound and picked up some of the soft dirt. "Better this than a dead horse," she said to Arlene. Mom poured the dirt onto a bright red spot. The blood vanished, then seeped out alongside the dirt.

I guess that's when I knew it was no use.

"Oh, Nipper! Nipper!" Arlene sounded shocked. I think she knew it was no use too.

Nipper had stopped struggling so hard. Arlene crouched by his head, holding him down. I turned away from his wild, frightened eyes. I picked up dirt and began sprinkling it on the cuts I could see. But I knew most of them were under the horse, where the tangled wire still cut into his flesh.

"We've got to have a vet," Grandad said, straightening up. He was a mess. He glanced at Mom. "Drive carefully, but hurry!"

Mom hurried to the car, turned it around, and sped off toward town. No one else drove by. Things got very quiet.

The gelding got quieter and quieter.

Arlene was crying. She had her face pressed against Nipper's neck. "Oh, Nipper! Nipper!" That's all she said. Over and over. In a whisper. My face was wet too, I realized then.

Grandad gave a long, slow sigh and stood up. He and the horse were a mass of blood and mud. He caught my eye.

Slowly, he shook his head.

CHAPTER 7

Accusations

WE DIDN'T get to church that morning. By the time the veterinarian arrived with Mom and we got home to clean up, it was too late for services. It was also too late for Nipper. He died two weeks later of lockjaw.

Arlene took it very hard.

At one time, I would have too. As it was, I felt very sorry for Arlene and Nipper. The three of us had been a lot of places together. We'd had a lot of fun. But I had Cheetah now to ease my hurt.

"Come and see my horse anytime," I told Arlene, hoping that would help.

She just sniffed and rubbed her red eyes.

June turned into July. I got a baby-sitting job four hours a day with a young couple's two cute children a mile down the road from us. It didn't pay much, but I didn't lose too much time from being with Cheetah. And it paid for the oats and hay I needed for her.

Ted Dunbar rode up one day in mid-July. He sat easily on Sinbad. The stallion whistled and snorted.

I laughed. "Cheetah's just ignoring Sinbad," I pointed out. The mare stood at the far end of the corral, idly switching flys in the shade.

"Her time will come," Ted said knowingly. "Sooner or later, ol' Sinbad causes all their hearts to flipflop."

"What brings you by here?" I asked. I was still mad about the time he'd tried to rope Cheetah without permission. And I still wondered if he had been responsible for the gate being opened that night. Grandad said it was "pure coincidence" that Nipper's and Cheetah's gates had been left open the same night, but in my anger I could imagine almost anything about Ted.

"I just rode by Arlene's again," Ted answered my question. "She's still taking it pretty hard."

"Something funny about that," I said darkly.

"Something funny about what?" he asked.

"Nipper getting out. His gate was open, you know. Nobody at Jonsson's seems to know how it happened."

Ted waited until the stallion's screams had quieted. "Gates get left open all the time," he said.

"That's what's so funny," I explained. "Our gate was unlocked that night too."

"It was? Same time?" He acted surprised.

"The night before Nipper got out I just happened to be near Cheetah's pen when the gate swung open. She made a run for it, but I scared her out of six weeks' growth. She might have been the one that got all tangled up instead of Nipper."

"Too bad you can't train a horse just to stand still when he gets tangled in barbed wire," Ted commented.

I remembered something Grandad had said about that. A horse in wire almost always goes crazy with fear. But Grandad had once owned a gelding that was wire-wise.

Even as a yearling, the horse would stand still for hours when he got his feet in wire. Somebody would get curious about why he stood so long in one spot, and they'd find him tangled in wire. I wondered what Cheetah would do if she ever got caught in barbed wire. I shuddered, thinking of how she might react.

"Ted, were you over at Arlene's the day before Nipper got out?"

"Me? No, why?"

"Oh, nothing."

"Come on, Karen! You're up to something, and I think I know what it is. You'd like to blame me for that open gate, wouldn't you?" Ted asked.

I didn't answer right away. I looked at Cheetah, standing calmly in the shade. She still wouldn't have anything to do with me or anybody else, but at least she was calmer now. "I wouldn't put it past you," I answered Ted's question.

"Thanks," he said sarcastically. "Thanks a lot, Karen." He turned the stallion around, facing the road. "I know you'll never believe me, but I was down at the river all that day, loading up cottonwood for winter firewood." He eased off on the reins and the chocolate-red stallion galloped away.

Grandad came out of the barn. He was carrying a halter he'd been repairing for the day when Cheetah would let us put one on her. I was surprised to see him. "I didn't know you were around," I told him with a nervous laugh.

"Kinda had your spurs raking high today, didn't you, Karen?"

"You mean Ted? He makes me mad."

"Obviously. But is that any reason to treat him so?"

"Somebody left the gate open at Arlene's, and Nipper got killed. My gate was opened the same night, and Cheetah tried to get out. I don't think it was coincidence that both gates were open."

"So you've decided that Ted is guilty?" Grandad asked.

"Well—yes."

"You surprise me, Karen. Really, you do." Grandad turned and walked back into the barn with the halter.

Something about the way he said those words hurt. I felt terrible. But I didn't know what to do or say, so I didn't say anything. I sighed and walked along outside the corral fence toward Cheetah. She turned her beautiful head and pricked up her ears, watching me alertly. But she didn't run!

"Cheetah," I told her, "sometimes I hate myself. But I always love you. But you don't seem to care." I stayed with the mare a while, then went inside to clean up my room. But the funny, unhappy ache inside stayed with me all the rest of the day.

Maybe that's why I felt rebellious that night at the family devotions Grandad always conducted when he stayed with us. He picked up his frayed, black-covered Bible, adjusted his bifocals well down on his nose, and began to read.

Mom knitted automatically as he read. When he handed the Bible to her, she read on without missing a beat. But when the Bible came to me, I had to be shown the place. I hadn't heard a word.

Even with Mom's finger on the verse, I couldn't focus my mind.

We didn't have a regular family altar in our home when just Mom and Dad were there. Only when Grandad came. I figured that Grandad must have always held evening family devotions in his home. That meant they had been part of Mom's life.

Then she'd married Dad. I'd heard how he used to sit on the church steps, waiting for her to come out of services or prayer meeting or choir practice. During the three years they had "courted," as they called it, Dad had never gone inside the church. Except on their wedding day. Then Dad hadn't gone back inside for years and years.

Mom had gone alone at first. Later she'd taken my older brothers and sisters—then me. But one day Dad made a public confession of Christ, and after that he went to church. But we never had family devotions.

Grandad's voice reached through my fog. "Are you listening, Karen?"

I raised my head, aware that my finger was on the verse where Mom's finger had been. But I still hadn't seen any part of it. "Grandad, I'm sorry for what I said about Ted today."

His blue eyes, so sober a moment before, burst into sparkling lights behind the bifocals. "Being sorry is a step in the right way, honey. Repentence comes first, you know."

"I'm sorry in a funny kind of way," I explained. "I hate myself for being so suspicious. But if Ted did have anything to do with those gates being left open, then it could happen again. And maybe this time I wouldn't be as lucky as before."

"But if Ted wanted to buy the mare he certainly wouldn't want her to get out and maybe get killed, would he?" Grandad asked.

"Maybe he'd do anything to keep me from having her," I said miserably.

"There!" Grandad said. "You've done it again: showed what you're really thinking—after confessing your sorrow over those thoughts. Now if you'll just look under your fingertip, you'll see what your mother and I have been reading. Paul had something to say about the very kind of thing that's bothering you. Read it. Romans 7:15."

I focused on the verse. "For that which I do, I allow not: for what I would, that do I not; but what I hate, that do I."

Mom looked up at me. "That's a bit confusing."

"More than a bit," I said.

"Not really," Grandad replied. "Paul's talking about sin. That's what makes us want to do one thing and end up doing another."

I stirred, a little uneasy. I didn't want a sermon. Yet I didn't want to keep on feeling guilty, either. The safest thing was to change the subject. "What caused you to become a Christian, Grandad?"

His eyes sobered again. He pushed the glasses back up on the bridge of his nose. "Sometimes a man's spiritual progress can be counted in the troubles he has. In fact, most people tend to ignore God until they get into something they can't handle. Or so it seems, anyway."

Mom pursed her lips. "There's something about that in Psalm 119:71, I think it is."

Grandad nodded. " 'It is good for me that I have been afflicted; that I might learn Thy statutes,' " he quoted. "Of course, most of us don't want to go that route: We don't want troubles and we don't want to learn of God. But sometimes, the only way we'll listen is through troubles."

That kind of talk made me uneasy. "You started out to tell me about when you were converted, Grandad."

"I was coming to that. It's hard to do sometimes, but I try to thank God for my hard experiences, especially when I can look back and see how they've helped me learn more about God's ways."

Mom smiled at me. "What your grandfather is leading up to, dear, is that he got himself in trouble before he found Christ."

Grandad nodded. He took off his glasses and set them upside down on the lamp table. He leaned back in his chair. "It was because of a near tragedy that I suddenly saw myself as I was—a man separated from God. Your grandmother told me I was too good a man for Christ to lose, but if it hadn't been for that close call—" His voice trailed off.

Mom said, "The way my mother told it to me, your grandfather was working in an irrigation ditch, all by himself, with a Fresno scraper and a team of mules when he gave his heart to Christ."

"Well, that's when it started," Grandad corrected Mom. "Something happened to frighten the team. I never was sure what, but anyway, they got scared and started to jump and kick, tangling the harness something awful."

"Did they run away?" I asked.

"Not really," he said. "I was able to hold them. But they twisted that big scraper in such a way that it caught my foot. I went down, hard, trapped under that weight and with those mules trying to go in 10 different directions at once."

Mom picked up the story. "He could have been killed —trampled by the mules or crushed by the scraper. No one was around. Anyway, nobody could see what was happening at the bottom of that irrigation ditch."

"What happened?" I asked Grandad.

"I prayed."

"What'd you say?" I asked.

"Just three words: 'Lord, help me!' "

"Did He?"

"I'm still here," Grandad stated simply.

"The truth is," Mom said with a faint smile, "those mules quieted down and your grandfather got them pulling together so the scraper moved off his foot. Then he unhitched the team and went home."

"Is that all?" I asked Grandad.

"No." He picked up his glasses, settled them in place and took the Bible from me. "That was just the turning point. I got to thinking about what could have happened. I started searching this Book." He held up the Bible. "It took some reading, because I wasn't familiar with God's Word. Oh, sure, we'd always had a Bible in the house, and your grandmother read it regularly and tried to get me to read it. But I wouldn't—until the day of the accident. Your grandmother was helping a sick neighbor or something, so I just muddled through."

"And that's how you became a Christian?" I asked.

He nodded. "I know people who try to make it very complicated, but really, God's plan of salvation is very simple."

I had heard a zillion sermons, I suppose. I knew the basics of becoming a Christian, I thought. Apparently Grandad read my thoughts, for he put down the Bible and looked at me over the top of his glasses.

"If that had been your friend out there on the roadway instead of her horse," he said, "could you have helped her find Christ on short notice?"

"Arlene's already a Christian," I said.

"OK, but supposing she wasn't. Or suppose it was Ted."

I felt my resentment seeping back. "I don't see what difference it makes, Grandad."

"I'm simply asking if you know the way to become a Christian, or to help someone find Christ. Could you do that, Karen?"

I was uncomfortable. "Sure," I said. "I've been to church all my life. I know the answers."

Grandad smiled tolerantly. "I'm reminded of a man peeling and eating an orange. Another man watching, who hasn't ever tasted an orange, thinks he knows what the first man's orange is like. Do you understand what I'm saying, honey?"

"Sure," I said flippantly. I'd had enough. "You want me to read some more?"

Grandad and Mom exchanged glances, and Grandad handed me the Bible. "Please do," he said.

I was glad when devotions were finally over and I was in bed. I looked up at the dark ceiling and thought about God.

I thought I was a Christian, yet I had never really accepted Christ. I didn't argue with God, and I tried to do right, generally. Still, I was sure I wasn't born again. Nothing had changed in my life. It was very confusing.

Outside, Cheetah whinnied. I raised up on one elbow and listened. I'd come to recognize the meaning of various sounds she made. This was different. I rolled out of bed, slid into my jeans, and padded silently through the house to the back door.

The yard was quiet. There was no moon. Still, by starlight, I could see Cheetah standing alertly in the corral, her neck over the fence. She was looking toward the river.

She whinnied again; that strange, unfamiliar whinny I hadn't heard before. It bothered me.

I stepped quietly onto the back porch to see better. I started to reach for the light switch. Then I stopped, my hand halfway to the switch.

Had I seen someone move in the shadows by the barn? Someone by the wire fence that used to shuttle the cows from the barn to the pasture by the river?

If I snapped on the light, whoever it was would run before I got a look at him. Gently, I pushed open the screen door and stepped out into the hot summer night.

Once again Cheetah called.

I ran, Indian footed, toward where I thought I'd seen someone in the night.

CHAPTER 8

Cheetah Makes Progress

I WOULDN'T have been surprised to see Ted Dunbar break out of the shadows and run. But I had only taken a few steps when the outside lights scattered the darkness. I turned around.

Grandad stood in the back door, his right hand shading his eyes from the sudden flare of the two large bulbs. "What's going on?" he called.

Quickly I spun to look where I thought someone had moved.

But no one was there. No movement. Nothing—except Cheetah's glossy neck lifted across the fence, her big brown eyes watching me. Grandad called again.

"I thought I saw someone out here and decided to take a look. But it's all right," I assured him.

Grandad came into the soft glow of the outside lights. He had pulled on his trousers but his pajama top flopped loosely about his shoulders. "You're sort of jumpy, aren't you, Karen?"

"A little, I guess." I walked over to the corral and

checked the bolt and wire loop. Each was secure. Reassured, I called pleasantly to the mare and walked back toward Grandad.

"Young lady," he said firmly, glancing at my feet, "you know better than to walk around a horse corral without shoes! You want to get lockjaw?"

"I know a girl who's gone barefooted around her corral for years, and she never had any trouble," I said.

"I don't care what your friends do, but I do care what you do! You go out barefooted once more and I'll withdraw my support of your mare. It's foolish and dangerous to walk around here like that. Is that clear?" Grandpa's voice was edged with irritation.

But he was right, and I knew it. "I'm sorry, Grandad. I won't do it again."

"Good. Now wash up and get to bed!" He sounded and looked funny without his false teeth.

"I sure thought I saw somebody out there," I said as I paused by the back porch to brush the soles of my feet.

"You're getting too spooky. You get washed up while I go make sure your mother's not upset about all this commotion."

Arlene Jonsson rode her bike over at about 10 A.M. the next day. I had been sitting patiently for an hour or so, watching the mare debate whether or not to eat some oats from a bucket I'd set about 15 feet in front of me. At the sight of Arlene, Cheetah's ears went up. She turned and frisked away to the far end of the corral.

"Hey!" Arlene called, climbing up to sit on the top rail of the corral, "it looks as if you're making some progress!"

"Well, she seems to know I'm no monster about to eat her alive, but she still won't let me get close. And no matter how hungry she gets, she always outwaits me."

"You'll win her over," Arlene declared from her high perch.

I approached her. "How're you doing, Arlene?"

"Fine. Dad says I can have another horse. But you know, I don't want one. No horse could replace Nipper. Not now, anyway. Maybe someday. But even then, it would have to be a special horse. Like Cheetah."

I glanced up at Arlene. A funny feeling came over me. I couldn't explain what it was.

Arlene's somber mood seemed to have passed. She was her usual cheery self. "How's the strategy going?" she asked.

"I've been thinking about trying to tighten up her space. I wanted to do it a long time ago, but Grandad talked me out of it. He was right—then. But now—"

"You figure that maybe you could get closer to her if she was in a smaller pen, like in that corner by the trees?"

I nodded. "If I could work closer to her, maybe I could get a halter on her. Once that's done, I think she'll let me pet her. Maybe even let me begin picking up her feet and other things like that. Think it'll work?"

"Maybe. She does seem a little calmer. Even though she ran when I came up, she didn't fly away full tilt. And she didn't try to climb the fence at the far end to get away from me." Arlene jumped down into the corral.

I explained my plan. If I nailed two long boards from the last tree to the fence, that would make three sides of a box, counting the back corner and side of the pen under the eucalyptus trees. "When she gets used to standing in that small space, we'll wait a few days, then close in the pen behind her."

"I get it. It'll be like having her in a loading chute!"

I nodded. "I can hardly wait to stroke her velvety neck. I'll bet she's as smooth as she looks. As smooth as Nipper—" I stopped, my foot obviously in my mouth. "I'm sorry, Arlene. I wasn't thinking."

"It's OK." She looked at the corner where I planned to build the pen. "She'll kick the boards down when we put them behind her."

"That's a chance we'll have to take."

"A kicking horse is useless," Arlene reminded me.

"She won't kick," I said. "Come on. Let's get started on that chute."

I found some 2″ x 12″ boards in the barn and we set to work, hammering away with the skill we'd developed as ranch girls who were natural tomboys. Cheetah stood in the far corner, wanting to come to the shade from the hot late July sun, but afraid to come near us. Still, she did not pace excitedly in spite of our hammering and sawing. She didn't whirl and race away, either. I grinned happily.

It was three days after we put up the side rails that Cheetah finally entered the chute. She smelled the new boards carefully, and rolled her eyes. But finally she went in, sniffing and snorting.

I was delirious with anticipation. In a few days, when she was thoroughly used to the shady chute, Arlene and I would slip the boards behind her, boxing her in. Then we'd just let her stand a while. Say several days. One day I'd walk up slowly, reach through the fence, and touch that velvet hide.

Arlene stood with a big grin on her face when she saw Cheetah switching flys in the chute. "She's making progress, Karen! Real progress."

I nodded happily. Cheetah had not run when Arlene pedaled up. The mare's ears were up, and she was alert to our every movement, but she was not alarmed. "She's too smart to rush out into this blazing August sun," I said, laughing.

"Has she let you walk up along the outside rails?" Arlene asked. "We'll have to work from there to put the back rails in, you know."

"I remember. No, she won't let me do that yet. She backs out when I come close."

"We've got to wait a while longer then," Arlene said. Her eyes were shining. "But it's worth it. What a horse!"

I glanced sharply at Arlene. Her admiration for Cheetah was obvious. Ted wanted my mare for the same calm, impersonal reasons his father bought and sold mares and their colts out of Sinbad. But Arlene had a different feeling for Cheetah.

I suppose I should have been glad. But I wasn't.

We sat in the shade of the tankhouse and watched the mare. It was too hot to do much else.

"Summer'll soon be over," Arlene observed. "School will start."

"But before school starts," I said, "my father will be home and—"

"You'll make it," Arlene said. "When he comes home, Cheetah will be tame enough so he won't make you get rid of her."

I glanced at her. That uneasy feeling welled up inside me again. Arlene was becoming *very* fond of my horse.

I changed the subject. "Say, Arlene, since you're a Christian, tell me something."

"What?"

"Recently, my grandfather asked if I knew the steps to becoming a Christian. I thought I did but I'm not really sure."

"Well, I'm not much at witnessing," Arlene replied, "although the pastor says that's just a way of saying 'I'm chicken' because opportunities to witness come daily."

"Well, just tell me what's necessary to become a Christian," I prompted.

"I guess you know the basic message of the Bible," she began.

"Sure," I said, "God loves us—John 3:16 and all that."

Arlene nodded. "OK, God loves us. That's why He sent His Son to earth—as a gift of love for us all."

"What's next?" I asked.

"Well, you know about sin, don't you? Sin separates us from God."

"I have trouble with that, Arlene. I never felt much like a sinner."

"But 'all have sinned, and come short of the glory of God,'" she quoted. "The sin of disobedience wrecked Adam and Eve's lives, you know. And we commit all kinds of sins."

"But, Arlene, I don't break any of the commandments or anything like that."

She looked at me with a little smile. "Funny you should say that."

"Why?" I demanded.

"Because you spend every waking second with that mare. She's first in your life."

I looked hard at my friend. "In other words, you're saying that Cheetah is more important to me than anything else?"

"Isn't she?" Arlene asked.

"In some ways, yes," I admitted.

"You know the first commandment is 'Thou shalt have none other gods before Me,'" she added.

"Cheetah's not a god to me!"

"She's first in your life, isn't she?"

"Don't be funny, Arlene!"

"I'm not trying to be! You asked me to explain about becoming a Christian, and I'm trying to do that."

"You're getting way off base!" I cried.

Arlene lowered her eyes. "I didn't mean to make you angry, Karen."

"I'm not!" I cried.

Arlene didn't answer, and just then Cheetah nickered softly. I glanced at her. Her ears were up and she was looking toward the road. Ted Dunbar was loping up the long driveway on Sinbad. The proud-stepping stallion began calling loudly to Cheetah. The mare answered. Ted held Sinbad firmly in check while he continued to trumpet to my horse. She stayed in the shade, alertly watching us.

"Sitting in the shade loafing, I see," Ted joked.

"I was just trying to get up enough energy to ride my bike home," Arlene replied. She stood up. "Well, see you," she said to me. She waved to Ted.

I didn't want her to leave just yet. I felt that we'd had a quarrel, and she was my best friend. And I certainly didn't want to stand there alone and talk to Ted Dunbar, especially after our last meeting.

"Stick around, Arlene," I called.

She shook her head, waved again, and pedaled off on her bicycle.

Ted was having trouble keeping the stallion from dancing out of the tankhouse shade toward the corral. "What were you two talking about?" he asked.

"You wouldn't be interested," I said.

He shrugged and looked at the holding chute. "You

plan to put boards behind her sometime when she's in that thing, right?"

I nodded.

"She'll kick you into the middle of next week."

"I don't think so," I said.

He had to speak to the stallion. Then he said, "Arlene left in kind of a hurry, didn't she?"

"Well, if you must know, we were talking religion," I replied.

"That's a good way to break up a friendship."

"Then maybe you and I should talk religion," I replied sarcastically.

"To tell you the truth," Ted said, tightening the reins and swinging the stallion back into the shade, "I'd like to know more about religion. Christianity, anyway."

I looked suspiciously at him, but he met my eyes evenly. "Why don't you ask my grandfather then?" I said.

"Maybe I will," Ted said. "In the meantime, I came over to ask if you're still determined to get killed, trying to tame that wild mare?"

"Meaning you still want to buy her—or rather, steal her?"

"She's a mighty fine looking brood mare, I think," he said. "But I still say it'll take a strong hand to break her."

"And I still say I'll break her my way!" I retorted.

"No need to get uppity, Karen," he said. "I'm just trying to keep you from getting hurt, that's all." He turned the stallion, then checked him again. "Don't think from what I said about wanting to know more about God and religion that I'm going to stand up in church and make a fool of myself or anything like that. I'm just curious, that's all." He let the stallion have a loose rein, and they loped toward the road.

"Grandad," I said after supper that night, "how can you tell if the Holy Spirit is moving?"

He and Mom exchanged glances. Grandad lowered his Bible and peered at me over the top of his glasses. "Oh," he said thoughtfully, "it's hard to say exactly. Why?"

I thought of what both Arlene and Ted had said today and how I'd behaved. "Oh, nothing special," I said to Grandad. I didn't want to discuss it, and neither Mom nor Grandad pushed me.

The next night Mom asked, "How's the mare doing?"

"She won't eat out of my hand or anything like that," I said. "But she doesn't run from me anymore, either."

"Sounds like progress," Mom said.

"She'll come around," I replied. "I know she will. I love her so much." I stopped, thinking of what Arlene had said about Cheetah and me and the first commandment.

Grandad asked, "Something I've been intending to ask, Karen. Any way of knowing if your mare might be going to have a colt?"

The idea startled me. "No, I guess not. Why?"

"Just curious—but if she's not with foal now, she probably will be interested sooner or later."

"There's no need to worry about that," I said with a chuckle. "She always turns a deaf ear to Sinbad."

"OK," Grandad replied. "I just wanted to remind you." He opened the Bible and adjusted his glasses again. "Anybody have a subject to throw on the table?"

Mom shook her head.

I thought a moment. "Yes," I said. "Arlene and I were talking about how to become a Christian, a real, born-again Christian."

Grandad looked at me over the top of his bifocals. "And you'd like some Bible references, huh?"

"I guess so. Mostly because we got interrupted and she had to leave before we finished."

"Repentance is always necessary, of course," Grandad said, leafing through the Bible. "Because we're all sinners and sin separates us from God. You know that?"

I nodded.

"Both John the Baptist and Jesus called for repentance," he continued. "Romans 5:8 tells us, 'But God commendeth His love toward us, in that, while we were yet sinners, Christ died for us.'"

"I earned a pin for learning Scripture," I reminded him. "I even remember John 14:6: 'I am the way, the truth, and the life: no man cometh unto the Father, but by Me.'"

Grandad smiled and nodded.

"So what's next?" I asked.

"After repentance the next step is simple—accept Jesus Christ by faith as your sin sacrifice."

"That's not simple," I said. "It's the hardest part of all."

"True, in one sense," Grandad agreed, "because Christ never forces His way in. Here." He extended the Bible to me. "Find Ephesians 2:8 and 9."

I turned the pages and read: "'For by grace are ye saved through faith; and that not of yourselves: it is the gift of God: not of works, lest any man should boast.'"

Grandad asked, "Does that answer your questions, Karen?"

"I guess so."

Grandad leaned toward me. "I'm reminded of what the eunuch in Acts 8 said to Philip after his questions were answered concerning Scripture, 'See, here is water: what doth hinder me to be baptized?'"

"Oh, Grandad, you can't baptize people!"

"No, but I can ask people to accept Christ as personal Saviour. And I'd be wrong if I didn't ask you to do that now: will you accept Him, Karen? Will you open your heart and let Him in?"

I shook my head. "I didn't want to know those things for myself, exactly, just for information generally, that's all."

Grandad seemed hurt. He slowly leaned back in his chair. "I see."

"Well, anyway," I said lamely, trying not to look at him or Mom, "I'm not ready."

Grandad said softly, "Meaning there are more important things in your life right now?"

I glanced sharply at him. He sounded like Arlene.

Outside, I heard Cheetah nicker. What was wrong with loving her? Love was what the Bible was all about. I felt uneasy, just the same. I wondered if Grandad was thinking the same thing Arlene had mentioned—that I had put Cheetah ahead of God—and thereby had broken the first commandment.

CHAPTER 9

Love Reaches Out

THE NEXT MORNING, Cheetah made her first trusting move toward me. It was just a little thing, but it was important.

I had given her oats and hay the night before. No feed was left in her manger when I came out at dawn. "Well, now," I told her, "we can't have that, can we? Let's see what's on the menu this morning for a beautiful horse."

Cheetah nickered softly when I came through the gate with a pitchfork of oat hay. I shoved the gate closed with my hips and slid the bolt into place with the back of my hand. My eyes went back to the mare. That's when it happened.

Slowly, cautiously, she moved toward me.

Hardly able to breath, I inched the fork toward her outstretched neck and head. Her ears were forward. Those hugh brown eyes watched me. Every muscle in that glistening body was taut. But she was moving toward me!

"Come on, ol' gal," I urged her, "come on! Eat some

hay right off your own personal pitchfork. Keep coming.
Keep coming. That's it!"

Her quivering nostrils were just inches from the hay.
Her lips were about to touch the feed. Then her nerve
broke. She snorted in sudden fright, almost turned herself inside out to wheel about, then thundered away to
stand blowing and wide-eyed in the far end of the corral.

I wanted to bawl. Then I realized how much progress
that action represented. *I was about to be accepted!*
Happily, I ran to the house to tell Mom and Grandad.

The second big event came two days later. I entered
the corral with a bucket of oats. I was hoping Cheetah
would try to eat from the pail. Slowly, tensely, the mare
approached. She was so keyed up, all her muscles quivered. Still, she kept coming, very slowly, toward my
outstretched arm.

Her nose touched the bucket. Just touched it. Again
her fear overcame her hunger. She whirled away. But
she only ran halfway down the pen. She stopped, faced
me with head up, then nickered softly.

Although she never would come back to the bucket I
kept holding out for her, I wasn't unhappy. On the con-
trary, I was thrilled. Things were going great.

Even her restlessness throughout much of the day did
not bother me. She peered over the fence toward the
river. She called again and again. I heard no answer but
figured she was whinnying to the mares and their growing
foals, roaming there.

"Grandad," I announced that night, after recounting
my near victory with the oats, "she'll be eating out of
my hand within a week."

"Wouldn't be surprised," he said, smiling. "Wouldn't
be surprised at all."

Arlene came over the next day. Neither of us said anything about the way our last meeting had ended. Instead, we both pounced on the one thing that was new: Cheetah stood quietly in her small chute while I looked through the fence at her from just a few feet away.

"Hey, would you look at that?" Arlene said as she got off her bike. "Think she'll run if I come close?"

The mare's ears swiveled toward my friend. Cheetah was curious, but didn't seem alarmed. "Come on over, but very slowly."

Twice Cheetah started to back out of the chute, but both times she changed her mind. When Arlene reached me, the mare stood, trembling and watchful, but still in the same place.

"Make a mark on the wall for this day," Arlene said, as she made a mark in the air.

"She's sure been restless the last few days," I said.

"Doesn't seem restless now," Arlene commented.

"Too hot in the middle of a day like this to get out of the shade, I guess," I said. "She just dances up and down in front of that far fence, stretching her neck across the top rail and calling to the mares down by the river. At least, I guess that's what she's doing."

"Well, she can be restless all she wants in this corral. If she couldn't get out when she came here, wild as a wolf, she certainly can't get out now. How about closing in the chute today?"

"Why not?" I replied.

We worked slowly, not wanting to frighten the mare.

"Seems to me," I whispered as we began to slip the first long board behind Cheetah's hind legs, "that we'd better just let this board sit lightly in place until we see what reaction she'll have."

"Right."

Cheetah turned her head curiously to watch us. We moved carefully, inching the board through the outside corral fence toward the slot made to receive it on the inside chute fence we'd built.

"Easy, Arlene," I hissed once. "You're shoving the board too fast and I'm getting a handful of splinters."

"Can Cheetah get slivers off the board if she backs up?" she asked.

"Not unless she shoves it sideways, as you're doing," I told her.

Arlene chuckled. The board eased off.

"There!" I said triumphantly a few minutes later. "It's done!"

The board was about halfway between the mare's hock and fetlock. Now all we had to do was wait to see how Cheetah would react to the first board.

"Be ready to yank it out fast if she panics," I warned.

Arlene said nothing, but I felt her fingers trembling beside mine on the end of the experimental board. "Do you really think she'll panic?" Arlene whispered.

"No," I replied honestly. "If I did, I wouldn't do this. Say, why are we whispering?"

We looked at each other and began to laugh. The unusual sound startled Cheetah. She nickered uncertainly and backed up. The back of her right leg touched the board we'd put up. Instantly, the leg flashed back in a kick. But the hoof was low, and the edge of the board caught Cheetah hard at the ankle.

"Ouch!" Arlene said for the mare. "That hurt!"

Instantly the mare sprang forward. Her forefeet went up, pawing at the end of the chute, away from the thing which had hurt her hind leg. Cheetah stood on her hind legs, raking the chute in front of her and whinnying in fear.

Arlene jumped up. "She's going over!"

"Quick! Help me pull that board out before she breaks a leg!"

This time we both got splinters in our hands as we frantically pulled the board out again. Then I stood up and called calmly to the mare. "Easy, Cheetah! It's all right!"

The mare turned to look at me. I saw fear in her huge brown eyes. She danced momentarily on two hind legs, still striking the front boards with her forefeet. Then she backed up half a step and came down on all fours.

I sighed with relief. "Good, girl! Good! It's all right!"

Cautiously peering backward, the mare backed out of the chute. When she was free, she threw up her head and tail and raced up and down the corral.

Arlene made a disgusted sound. "Another setback!"

"Maybe not. She had a moment of fear but she didn't really try to go over the front fence after that first reaction. And look! She's already stopped bolting around the corral!"

Arlene laughed. "Well, that may be, but she's sure going to blow a gasket if she keeps blowing like that."

I pulled at the slivers in my hands. "Did you notice she didn't kick the second time?" I said. "She's smart."

"I thought she had wings the way she dove forward and tried to go over that fence. She almost went crazy," Arlene said.

"She's not crazy!"

"Now don't get yourself in an uproar again!" Arlene said. "Honestly, Karen, I don't know why you get upset so easily! I just meant 'crazy' as a figure of speech."

"I'm sorry, Arlene. I don't know what gets into me. Well, yes, I do. If I believe what Grandad says."

We watched Cheetah a moment as she stretched her neck across the top of the corral and gazed toward the river. She let out a long whinny.

"What does your grandfather say?" Arlene asked.

"He quoted Paul about doing what he didn't want to do."

"Your grandfather is pretty smart, Karen. You know he led the barber to Christ last week, don't you?"

"The town barber?" I was surprised. "But I heard he was an alcoholic. I know I used to smell liquor on his breath when he cut my hair."

"I hear he hasn't had a drink since he prayed to receive Christ. And your grandfather led him to Christ while getting a haircut!"

"You're kidding!"

Arlene held up her right hand in a solemn manner. "I was never more serious. And you know what else I heard? That the barber was just waiting for someone to explain Christ to him. But nobody ever did."

"That's hard to believe," I said.

"Ask your grandfather."

"He never says anything about what he's done for the Lord. Only talks about what is left undone. I know he led three others to Christ this summer, but he never told me. I learned about it at church. Right now, he's after me and Ted Dunbar."

"Ted? No kidding," she said, smiling.

"Yes, he tried once. But you know, Arlene, a funny thing happened after that. Ted later told me he'd like to know about Christ. But I thought he was just kidding me, trying to soft-soap me."

"Why did you think that?" Arlene asked.

"Because Ted's always kidding around."

"I wonder—" Arlene began. "Ted's pretty popular at school. I wonder what would happen to this town if he turned his life over to Christ."

"That'll never happen," I said.

"Do I have your personal guarantee on that?" Arlene said, half smiling.

She was my best friend, but she could get on my nerves sometimes.

I glanced at Cheetah. She was pacing up and down the river-side fence rails, ears cocked. I didn't like her restlessness.

"Tomorrow," I said to Arlene, "if she goes back into that chute, I'll bet I get to touch her."

"I hope you're right," Arlene said. "She's sure smelling or hearing something down by the river. But I can't see anything from here."

"Neither can I."

After devotions that night, Grandad walked out to the barn. Restless, I followed him out but headed for the corral to check on my horse. "What's the matter, Cheetah?" I asked her through the gate. "What do you smell or hear down there by the river, hmmm?"

Cheetah ignored me. She kept her ears cocked toward that invisible attraction. I opened the gate and stepped inside the corral, sliding the bolt behind me. "What is it, Cheetah?" I said.

The mare turned briefly to look at me, then returned to her vigil. However, she moved slowly away from me as I tried to approach. Apparently she was watching me out of the corner of her eye.

I checked her manger. She had hay and oats, also water

and her salt block. I shrugged, unable to figure out what
was troubling her.

"Karen!" Grandad's voice hit me with its urgency. I
straightened instantly, alarmed by the strained note in his
voice.

I saw him, leaning against the barn. He was hunched
over. A bridle lay on the ground in front of him where
he had dropped it. "What's the matter, Grandad?"

"Karen, ask your mother to come out here at once!" he
called.

"What's wrong?" I asked.

"Hurry!"

I leaped for the gate, opening and closing it quickly.
I threw the bar and sprinted for the house. The overhead
lights on the barn and tankhouse made dual shadows
which seemed to try outrunning me. "Mom! Mom!" I
called, slamming through the back screen door into the
kitchen. "Grandad wants you right away!"

Mom stepped away from the sink. She dried her hands
on her apron as we hurried back into the night. Grandad
was slumped on the ground, his back against the old barn.

"Better get the car," he said with great effort as we
reached him. "I don't feel too hot."

"What is it?" Mom demanded, kneeling beside him.

I saw the pain in his old face. "Get the car!" That's
all he said.

Mom ran to obey.

We rushed him to Riverbend and the small hospital
with its emergency room. I'd been there once when I
broke my collarbone after a neighbor's horse fell on me.
During the fast ride through the hot summer night,
Grandad lifted his seamed old face to me. He spoke with
difficulty. "It's hard to see what the psalmist meant about

being good to have been afflicted—" he grimaced, breaking off the sentence.

I reached out, wanting to ease his pain, but I couldn't help him.

Mom kept her eyes on the road, driving fast through the quiet summer night.

When he could speak again, Grandad continued his thought. "Trouble is for growing," he whispered. "Wonder what lesson—?" Again the pain cut him off.

Then we were at the hospital. The emergency room staff took over and quickly phoned the doctor. Mom leaned weakly against the wall, shaking. I hugged her close, tears streaming down my cheeks.

We had done all we could. Half-aloud, Mother pleaded with God for Grandad until the nurse led us to a regular waiting area.

The doctor came to us there a long time later.

"We'll need to keep him overnight," he said, stuffing his stethoscope into one of the pockets of his short, white jacket. "We need to run some tests. You may as well go home. We'll call you when we know anything."

Mom said hopefully, "What is it? Indigestion?"

That's what Grandad had said it was when we got him into the car. Indigestion. But I didn't believe that. I didn't think Mom did either. She was just being hopeful.

"We'll know more in the morning," the doctor replied, ignoring Mom's speculation. "But I wouldn't send you home if I thought there was reason to stay here."

Mom and I grabbed on to those words with hope. We went into the night, shaken by the sudden turn of events. Neither of us said what I suspected we were both thinking: heart attack.

Instead, we drove back home silently. Mom turned into

our drive, and the car headlights swung across the yard as we circled toward our detached garage.

"Mom! Stop!" My sudden cry made Mom slam on the brakes in great alarm. She looked at me in surprise.

I pointed through the dust we'd raised. The headlights showed clearly Cheetah's sturdy board corral.

"Look! The corral gate's open! Cheetah's gone!"

CHAPTER 10

The Struggle Within

EVEN BEFORE the car was fully stopped, I threw open the door and ran frantically to the corral. The pen was empty and silent, just as I had feared.

I sprinted back to the car. "Mom! Cheetah's really gone!"

Mom's wan face was lit faintly by the glow of the car's instrument panel. "How'd she get out?"

"I must not have latched the gate properly when Grandad called. I didn't put the wire loop in place. She's one smart horse, you know. But that doesn't matter now. We've got to find her!"

Mom's voice was flat and low. "Honey, the most important thing right now is your grandfather."

"Mom! You said it was just a little indigestion! And you know what happened to Arlene's horse when he got out! Maybe Cheetah's out there on the highway right now! Let's go look for her!"

"Karen, I know how much that mare means to you," Mom said gently, "but Grandad needs our prayers."

"Cheetah might get killed!"

"And your grandfather might die."

Mom's frightening words punctured my own wild concern. I leaned my head inside the driver's window. "All right," I told her. "Let's pray."

We went inside and knelt to pray. The house seemed strangely empty tonight without Grandad. But now he was in the hospital. And outside, somewhere in the hot night, Cheetah was loose. Both lives might be in danger, I knew.

I don't remember praying. But we did. Mom and I urged God to spare Grandad and return him safely to us. And I added a prayer for Cheetah.

When we finally raised our heads, I noticed how red Mom's eyes were—the tip of her nose too. She patted her rumpled hair. "I want to read a while," she said. "You might phone Arlene and ask her to help you look for Cheetah."

It was late to phone anybody, but I had to find Cheetah, and I'd need help. Arlene's mother answered the phone. The sleep went out of her voice when I told her quickly about Grandad and Cheetah. Mrs. Jonsson called Arlene to the phone.

"I'm sorry about your grandfather," Arlene said after I'd blurted out my problem. "And I'm sorry about your horse. Can I help?"

"Do you have any idea where Cheetah might have gone?"

"Well, she was pretty restless tonight, looking toward the river—"

"Of course! I should have thought of that! She's probably joined Dunbar's brood mares and their colts!"

There was silence on the other end of the line for a

moment, then Arlene asked, "Did you look for tracks?"

"I didn't think of it."

"Listen," Arlene said, "I'll get dressed and come over with Mom and help you look."

I took the flashlight and checked the hard-packed dirt outside the corral. I couldn't see anything, except the mare's prints where she had escaped through the open gate.

I played the light along the fences—no sign of trampled wire. I sighed with relief. She must have escaped through the opening where a wire gate had once been. Dad hadn't replaced the gate after he had sold the cows.

Just past the wire fence, the flashlight showed a partial imprint of an unshod hoof. Cheetah had gone this way! I ran across the pasture, shining the light around and calling into the darkness. There was no sign of the mare.

When the flashlight batteries began to weaken, I turned back to the house. Arlene's mother drove in just as I opened the back screen door. Mrs. Jonsson went immediately to Mom and Arlene came to me. "Oh, you poor kid!" she said, putting her arm around me a moment.

"I found Cheetah's track in the pasture," I explained. "She didn't go to the highway."

"That's something to be thankful for. Have you got another flashlight for me?"

"No. And the batteries in this one are giving out. Have you got a light in the car?"

Arlene shook her head. "We can't do much without a light. How's your mom?"

"She's OK."

"Maybe we should go in with her?"

"No need. Your mother's with her."

Arlene looked at me sort of strangely. I knew what she

was thinking. "Well, maybe I'd better check up on her," I said.

Mom looked pale, but she was trying to smile for Mrs. Jonsson. "We're going to have prayer," Mom announced, then suddenly began to cry.

I ran to her and put my arms around her. She put her head on my shoulder. Her whole body shook.

For a long time, we stood that way.

When I looked up, both Mrs. Jonsson and Arlene were standing with bowed heads. Their lips moved. I felt funny. I felt guilty. Yet I wanted desperately to find Cheetah.

Mom sniffed and managed a weak smile for our visitors. "I'm sorry, Karen," she said to me. "I'll be all right. You and Arlene go find your horse."

"No," I said, fighting guilt, "I'll stay here with you."

"But your horse—"

"She went toward the river."

Mrs. Jonsson asked, "What's down at the river?"

"Brood mares and colts," I said.

"And Sinbad," Arlene said quietly.

Of course! Sinbad! Not the mares! Not the colts! But the proud-stepping stallion with gold highlights in his magnificent coat.

"Also," Arlene said quietly, "there are a bunch of wild hogs."

I glanced sharply at her.

Mom dabbed at her eyes. "The stallion won't let the hogs hurt your horse, Karen. But you certainly can't go down there. Absolutely not."

I felt fear rising inside. I didn't want Cheetah running loose, no matter how safe she might be or how dangerous it was for me to try getting her back.

Arlene seemed to read my thoughts. "There's one thing we could do now," she said.

"What's that?"

"Phone Ted Dunbar and ask him if he's seen Cheetah," she suggested.

"At this time of night?" Mom asked.

"Ted says he always stays up late," Arlene explained. "Besides, we need to know if he's got Sinbad penned up at the house. If he has, Cheetah may be where Ted can see her."

"And if the stallion's not penned up, and the mare isn't there," Mrs. Jonsson guessed, "that means they're together on the river bottom. Along with the wild hogs."

I had to know. I picked up the phone and called Ted. His voice was heavy with sleep. I had awakened him, but I didn't care. I had to know about Cheetah. Quickly, I told him why I'd called. "Is Sinbad loose?" I concluded.

"He hasn't been in the corral for a couple days or more. I've been letting him exercise by running free on that river bottom land."

I hesitated. Certainly Ted didn't owe me any favors. Still, I had to ask. "Could you take a light and see if Cheetah's around anyplace?"

"I don't have to look. Sinbad's been blasting out a love call all day. A while ago I heard two horses running down on the river, and he's quit calling. I thought one of our brood mares had gotten out and was running with him. But it has to be your mare."

I thought of the miles of unfenced land along the river and the tangles of cottonwood, willow, oak, wild blackberry, and grapevines. And the hogs. I tried to sound pleasant. "Do you think you could take a flashlight and see if they're anyplace close?"

Ted chuckled over the phone. "Well, now! Listen to who's being nice."

"Please, Ted?"

I guess that surprised him. His voice was serious in my ear. "I wouldn't dare go down on that river bottom at night any more than you would. Maybe those hogs won't hurt anyone, but I'm not going to give them a chance to prove otherwise. Besides, Sinbad wouldn't let anybody walk up to him when he's running free with a friendly mare." Again he chuckled. "And what makes you think anybody will ever catch that wild horse of yours with all that country to run in?"

I thanked him and hung up the phone. I felt terrible, and yet I felt better. Cheetah was safe with Sinbad. But she was also wild and free again. How in the world would I ever get close enough to catch her and pen her now? Things sure looked gloomy.

When I turned and saw my mother's face, my heart melted. "Mom," I said, putting my arms around her, "I've been terribly selfish. I'm so mixed up. I want to join you and Mrs. Jonsson and Arlene in prayer."

Mom's eyes filled with tears. She reached up and pulled me down beside her. I heard Mrs. Jonsson give a little sob. I felt Arlene's hand on my arm.

"God, forgive me," I whispered. "I'm so confused. Help Grandad! Ease his pain. Make him well again, if it's Your will. I love him so. And Cheetah. Protect her. I love her too. I don't know which way to turn. Please help me!"

I was crying by then. After a few minutes, Mrs. Jonsson and Arlene slipped out quietly and went home.

Eventually, I fell asleep on the couch, completely exhausted. The phone's jangle awakened me. I opened my eyes to see Mom still asleep in the chair where Grandad usually sat. I jumped up and answered the phone.

"This is the hospital," a woman's crisp voice said in my ear. "May I speak to Mrs. Keith, please?"

Mom was awake and alert now. I reached over and gave her the receiver. She listened tensely and said, "All right."

She gave me the phone to hang back up. "They want me to come," she said dully.

My spirits sank. "I'm going with you," I said.

That was one of the strangest rides. It was still dark and very hot, yet I shivered in the car. Mom drove fast, her beams high on the quiet, empty country road. We slowed for the tree-lined city streets, bounced into the hospital parking lot, then dashed into the building.

The doctor gave it to us straight. "He's having a pretty rough time of it. His heart."

Mom's shoulders sagged. I felt cold.

"May we see him?" Mom asked in a small, tight voice.

The doctor shook his head. "Not now. But I thought you might like to be close by. The chapel is open down the hall," he added, pointing.

It was a tiny chapel. Probably it had once been a storage area. An open Bible lay on a small altar. A white cross on the wall glowed from small lights behind it.

Mom and I slid into the first of three short pews. She began to pray aloud.

I couldn't, not then. My thoughts dipped and climbed, twisted and rolled. For the first time in my life, somebody dear to me was near death. Mom was taking it hard. Every now and then, her voice broke with a sob.

And I—well, I had been more concerned about my horse being loose. I felt terribly guilty. Yet I really loved that horse. I cared what happened to her. And I also cared what happened to Grandad, for I loved him too. It wasn't a matter of a choice between them. Obviously, Grandad was in the greatest danger. I should pray for him, but something kept me silent.

Was it wrong to love a horse so much, one I'd wanted so desperately all my life? I didn't love my grandad any less. I loved them both. Yet—somehow—I felt wrong about loving Cheetah.

I went to sleep in the pew, my head resting uncomfortably against the corner scroll. I didn't mean to sleep. I just put my head back to rest my eyes a moment while Mom prayed beside me.

The sound of sparrows chittering in the ash trees outside the chapel window aroused me. Mom was gone.

I jumped up, glanced quickly around the chapel, then hurried out into the hallway.

Mom was nowhere in sight. That scared me.

Quickly I walked to a desk. A nurse glanced at me. "The doctor came for your mother," she said. "She's with your grandfather."

"May I go in?"

She shook her head. "Doctor's orders. You're to stay here."

"But I can't just stand out here!"

"I'm sorry, honey," the nurse said. "Sometimes all anybody can do is wait."

Dejectedly I walked back to the chapel.

This time, I prayed.

CHAPTER 11

Trapped by Wild Pigs

"HAVING DONE ALL, to stand—" Paul's words to the Ephesians came to me some time later. I raised my head and opened my eyes. I had prayed for Grandad with all my heart. I had also prayed about Cheetah.

And I had reached a decision about the mare.

I left the chapel, now glowing with morning sunlight, and walked down the hallway toward the waiting room. Nurses were hurrying along and supply carts were being trundled down the hall. The hospital was tuning up for a new day.

I spotted Mom coming out of the swinging doors to the Intensive Care area. We hurried toward each other. I guess my fear showed in my eyes, for Mom started to smile a little, though she looked very tired.

"He's resting," she said immediately. "He's got a chance."

"Thank God," I breathed, as I threw my arms around her.

"Amen," she whispered.

Mom pulled back from my embrace and dabbed at her eyes. "The doctor says that if Dad doesn't have another attack, he should make it. But he'll be in the hospital at least six weeks, flat on his back."

Tears flooded my eyes. "The important thing is, he's going to get well. God has answered our prayers."

Mom explained, "You were sleeping so soundly when they came for me, I just let you sleep. Besides, there was nothing you could do. But I'm sorry I let you sit out here so long by yourself."

"Is Grandad awake?" I asked.

"He was. He sent a message to you," she said.

"To me?"

"He could barely speak, but he said to tell you that 'God loves you, and so does Grandad.'"

My tears fell freely.

Mrs. Jonsson, Arlene, and several other neighbors were waiting for us when we pulled into our driveway that morning. The neighbors pushed anxiously forward as our car bumped up the long dusty driveway.

I stuck my head out the car as we approached and yelled, "He's going to make it!"

You never heard such a hubbub.

The women gave glad little cries and pressed against the car the moment it stopped. They reached through the windows and kissed and hugged Mom and me. We were all bawling by the time we got inside our house. The place was spotless. There was food on the table and fresh-perked coffee smelled delicious. Neighbors! Neighbors who cared!

After a while, when Mom had told and retold all the details of that long night, Arlene motioned for me to follow her outdoors.

We walked slowly toward the empty corral. "I talked to Ted a little while ago," Arlene said. "He went down to the river and got Sinbad. Penned him up by their house."

I grabbed Arlene's shoulders and made her face me. "Cheetah? What about Cheetah?"

She wouldn't look at me directly. "Cheetah wasn't with him."

If she had slapped me in the face, I couldn't have been more surprised.

When she did look up there were tears on her eyelashes. "Oh, she had been with Sinbad. Ted found plenty of hoof prints. Cheetah's the only unshod horse around here, so there's no doubt about the tracks. Ted figures that when Cheetah heard him calling for Sinbad, she ran and hid someplace."

I thought about that possibility. I wasn't sure that she would hide, but she certainly would have run. "Ted didn't hear her?" I asked.

Arlene shook her head. She made a little squirming motion. Something about that action alarmed me again.

"What's the matter, Arlene?"

She lowered her eyes again. "There's one thing more."

"What?" I cried.

"I tried to follow Cheetah's tracks from here." Arlene waved her arm toward the pasture. "I remembered she couldn't get to the river without going through one more fence—the one that keeps Sinbad off your place."

I stared at Arlene. What was she leading up to?

"Cheetah tried to go over that fence, I guess." Arlene's voice quivered. "The top wire had been broken, and there was horsehair on it."

"Arlene, get to the point! Cheetah's hurt, isn't she?"

She nodded, meeting my eyes. "There's blood on the far side of the fence."

I sagged.

"There's one thing more," Arlene continued. "Ted also found blood on the unshod tracks near the river."

"How much blood?" I forced myself to ask.

"Enough so that we'd better find Cheetah soon."

We ran back to the house to tell our mothers where we were going. We didn't mention the blood and our urgency.

Mom patted me on the shoulder. "Of course, dear. But when you find her, come back and tell us. Don't try to catch her or anything like that."

Mrs. Jonsson added, "There's no need to. Perhaps I did the wrong thing, but I thought it was proper, so I called your father at the lumber camp and told him about the heart attack and all."

Mom smiled at me. "Your father's coming home. He'll be here in a few hours, and he'll have something to say about that wild horse."

BANG!

Just like that, my timetable for taming Cheetah was shot to pieces. I had expected to have her calmly leading at halter before he got home. Not that it mattered much anymore. Everything had gone wrong in the past few hours.

Well, not quite everything.

"Well," Arlene said, nudging me, "let's get going! Cheetah needs us."

I grabbed a double handful of oats from the sack and stuck them into an old brown paper sack. "Might help," I explained to Arlene. She nodded. Then we were off, dogtrotting across the pasture toward the river.

At the gate, we paused to examine the evidence.

It was just as Arlene had said. The top strand of barbed wire had been snagged, as Cheetah tried to jump it. Farther on there were brown bloodstains on the ground by the unshod hoof prints. Big brown stains.

Arlene stood up, glancing toward the river where the tracks led. "My guess is that she caught a piece of barbed wire on the right hind leg. And, from the way that hoof has been dragged in the dirt, I'd guess maybe the wire cut her between her hoof and ankle."

I nodded. "Looks that way." I didn't add that the injury might permanently cripple her, or mention what might happen if infection followed.

Arlene pointed. "That's where Ted said he caught Sinbad. Maybe we can pick up Cheetah's trail from there."

We jogged on. Soon we were pushing through tall, dry grass. Overhead the river oaks, cottonwoods, and willows made a canopy which filtered the sun. Wild grapevines and high, stickery mounds of blackberry vines climbed everywhere. We found Ted's, Sinbad's, and Cheetah's trails.

"Like a jungle in here," Arlene said finally, pausing for breath. "Maybe we should climb up one of those trees and look around."

I nodded, still puffing from our fast pace. "It's pretty hard going in here, and we're making so much noise she might run without us ever seeing her."

Arlene started to say something but closed her mouth with a snap and started to climb up the tangled, wild grapevines.

I guessed that she was thinking, *If Cheetah can still run.*

I sat down to catch my breath and accidentally put my hand on a stinging nettle. Little white bumps popped out on my hand even before Arlene called down to me.

"There she is!" She was pointing straight ahead. "Backed up against the river, under a big cottonwood!"

"Don't yell!" I whispered fiercely. "You might scare her away! Come on down!"

Arlene scrambled to the ground and brushed her hands. "She's back in the shadows so far, I almost didn't see her. But we're in luck. The blackberry vines are on two sides, and the river's behind her. She can drink from it but not cross because it's the deep part. Unless she'll try to swim."

"You think we can come in from the front and block her escape?" I asked, keeping my voice low.

Arlene frowned thoughtfully. "She may not try to run out. When she heard my voice, her head and ears came up, but she—she didn't try to stand."

We just looked at each other.

"I'd better go first," I said. "She's less likely to run from me—if she can run." We started off.

"What're you going to do when you get to her, Karen?"

I patted the right hip pocket of my blue jeans. "I'll try the oats."

"Better be ready to jump in case she tries to run over you."

I didn't answer, but pushed quietly ahead through the deep tangle of river weeds.

Arlene's hand lightly touched my back. I stopped, breathing hard from the rough going. Arlene whispered, "She's just past that clearing up ahead."

I nodded, spotting the opening and the blackberry vines beyond. The line of willows showed the river's edge beyond the vines. I bent forward to escape a drooping wild grapevine and took one step forward.

Suddenly, a startled hog sprang up from the cool shade and stood facing us. She was huge!

I nearly knocked Arlene down when I jumped back in surprise and alarm. "Wild sow!" I cried. "With pigs!"

I didn't have to tell Arlene to move. She turned and started to run. I was half a step behind her.

But the sow wasn't satisfied to have us run. I heard her angry squeal as she charged after us.

We both grabbed the nearest overhanging vines and swung ourselves up into a tree.

The sow clicked her teeth below us, gazing up with ugly little eyes. She was at least three feet long, reddish colored, with floppy, scarred ears.

"What a monster!" Arlene said, clinging to a limb.

"She meant business," I puffed. "I saw her pigs. I suppose she thought we were going to harm them."

"What now?" Arlene asked, gazing down at the sow as she ran around below us, squealing.

My fear of the hog began to ebb. Cheetah was just a little way ahead, probably weak from the effects of her wire cut. She needed help, if she'd let us help her—and if we could get to her.

"We could wait for the sow to go away," I said, "except that we don't dare. We've got to get to the mare."

"Past that mean-eyed hog?"

"Help me think of a way." I peered ahead, past the clearing, to the natural shelter where Cheetah was. I finally saw her, still lying down. Her head was up and her ears were cocked toward us. Why hadn't she run? I shuddered, thinking the worst.

"Arlene," I said, "I can see her from here. She's still lying down."

"That's good."

"No, that's bad. Normally, with all this noise, she'd be halfway to the next county by now."

Arlene's eyes met mine.

"She's down—down hard, I'd guess. Down and can't get up. I've got to get to her," I explained.

"How? Swing through the trees like Tarzan?"

I debated. "There's no way across that open space except on foot. But maybe I can work my way through these vines from here and outrun the sow across the clearing."

"Then what? How will you deal with the horse and sow at the same time?"

"You stay here. Maybe she won't follow me."

Arlene pursed her lips thoughtfully. "I've got a better idea. You go ahead on the vines. Sing out when you're at the edge of the clearing, ready to jump to the ground."

"What're you going to do?"

"Never mind," Arlene said. "You get moving."

I reached the clearing in a few minutes. But that took me closer to the little pigs. The sow came squealing after me, threatening me from below with all kinds of horrible things if I'd just come down from those vines. I felt the hair on my neck standing stiff as pins. Arlene stayed close behind me.

I turned around. "Now what?"

"Give me a second," Arlene whispered. I could hear the fear in her voice. "Now!"

Arlene started to climb down the vines.

"No!" I screamed. "No, Arlene!"

"You get to the horse," Arlene called back. She jumped with a yell. The sow gave an angry squeal and charged after her Arlene ran like she was possessed and vanished into the tall grass.

"Oh, God, help her!" I moaned.

Arlene shrieked back over her shoulder, "Run, Karen! Run!" Her voice faded fast in the underbrush and trees.

I obeyed, jumping the last few feet from the vines to the ground. I dashed across the open space, straight to Cheetah. She started up with a frightened whinny. Her right hind leg was drawn up toward her body.

"Easy, Cheetah! It's me!" I forced myself to stand still, half-crouched from my wild dash. "Easy, Cheetah!"

Behind me, a long way off, I heard Arlene's voice taunting the pig. Her voice sounded high, as though she were in a tree.

Cheetah gave a frightened whinny and bunched her body to run. Her only way to freedom lay past me.

CHAPTER 12

Love, the Miracle Worker

"EASY, CHEETAH! EASY!" I put all my feeling and urgency into those words.

The mare stood tensed, ears swiveled toward me, every muscle quivering. I could see little black BB-like rows of drying blood on her injured back leg. She had run through mud, and that had stopped the bleeding.

I kept talking while I looked over the mare's body. She was dirty and her hair and mane were matted with cockleburs and underbrush. She had triangular rips or tears in the flesh of both hind legs where she'd caught the barbs. There was a bigger wound near the right rear hock.

I figured she had cleared the fence with her beautiful body, but not her hind legs. The right one had probably broken the wire. It had curled back when released from the tension of the post and sliced into the fetlock, or maybe the pastern, between hoof and ankle. That was the bad cut—the one the mudcake had helped stop bleeding.

She must not run on that leg. Running could tear the wound open, and she would bleed again. Since she had not run at the sound of our voices, she obviously was in rough shape.

I kept talking softly, trying to keep her from bolting. The oats! I shook some into my hand and extended it. "Oats, Cheetah! Good oats!"

The untamed quality of her mind showed in her wide eyes, flaring nostrils, and short, fearful snorting. She was going to run! And no telling where she would go in that tangled river bottom.

"God, please!" The words escaped my lips.

I began to back up, very slowly. Cheetah made a startled sound and hobbled forward on three legs, but stopped immediately.

I figured her leg was hurting plenty.

Slowly, hopefully, I put the oats down in a little pile. "There," I said soothingly, "you can eat them off that big leaf if you won't take them from my hands."

Cheetah took another hobbling step toward me, still poised for flight. She ignored the oats.

"You don't need to be afraid, Cheetah," I said. "No, not of me. See? I won't hurt you. Not a bit." I continued to back up slowly. "Tell you what, Cheetah. I'm going to take a chance and sit down right here." And I sat down right at the opening of her natural pen. If I backed up, she could slip out. Where I was, she couldn't get out without running over me. "And you wouldn't do that, girl, would you?" I added, hopefully.

As I sat there, the sun burning my back through my shirt, the quivering slowly went out of the mare's taut muscles. Her ears slowly eased back to a less alert position.

"Tell you what, Cheetah," I said after a while, "just to show you there's no harm intended, I'll turn my back on you. See? Notice how very, very slowly I turn around? There!"

I listened, every fiber of my body tight as a watch spring. If I heard the sudden pounding of her unshod hooves, I'd have to jump for my life.

But there was no thunder of hoofbeats. Instead, Cheetah snorted noisily.

I waited a moment, then cautiously turned to look over my shoulder.

Her neck was outstretched. Her nostrils sucked in air and blew it out again with fluttering blasts. Then even that ceased.

Cheetah stood, her injured right rear leg drawn up slightly toward her body, watching me.

I sighed with relief, then began looking for Arlene. Or the wild sow. I strained to hear too, but the only sound across the clearing was the drilling of a woodpecker.

I was sick with concern.

Where was Arlene? I wanted to call but was afraid of scaring the mare. Still, what was the mare compared to my friend? I cupped my hands and began to call softly, "Arlene!"

Even though she didn't answer, I knew the sow hadn't gotten her. If it had, I'd have heard a commotion. Besides, I had heard her, taunting the hog. And she had sounded as though she were up in a tree again.

But where was she? I hoped she hadn't fallen. If anything had happened to her, it would be my fault. The whole complex problem began to bear down on me like some immense hand.

In fact, I suddenly felt as if everything were my fault.

Grandad was fighting for his life in the hospital, yet I had been more concerned with my horse's escape.

My horse! Everything had begun with that single desire to have a horse of my own.

How many unkind things had I said to Ted Dunbar because of my horse?

How close had I come to breaking up my friendship with Arlene over the mare? And I'd been glad it was my best friend's horse that died instead of mine.

What pain and hurt I must have given Grandad by putting Cheetah first in my life, instead of God.

Then there was the pressure of trying to keep Dad from knowing about Cheetah's wild nature. Now he was coming home early. I knew what he would say. Not that it mattered anymore. But I hadn't even touched Cheetah's beautiful glossy neck—not even once.

What was worse, she had escaped and hurt herself. Now she was down here on the river bottom, in need of help, and nobody could get near her. And Arlene—brave Arlene!

It didn't make sense. All I'd wanted to do was love that horse and have her love me. Instead, my whole world had come apart.

In that black moment, everything was wrong. And I felt totally helpless. I began to cry, my head on my drawn-up knees. I don't know how long I sat there, shaking with sobs, my face hidden from the hot afternoon sun.

I felt something touch my hip pocket.

I stopped sobbing, too exhausted emotionally to raise my head right away. What had touched me? Slowly, very slowly, I twisted my head, keeping my forehead on my knees, until I could see behind me.

Cheetah stood there, muzzle outstretched. She trembled. Nervous blasts came from her nostrils. But she was just inches behind me.

And she had touched me!

I had felt her nose touch my right hip pocket! The oats! She smelled the oats I had there!

Wordlessly and slowly—very slowly—I twisted my right arm back and carefully pulled out the paper bag. Cheetah blew noisily through flared nostrils and poised to run, but she stood her ground. The oats on the ground behind her were gone.

Slowly I raised my head and turned to face her, offering the new oats. Then I drew my arm back, emptied the oats into my right hand, and extended that to her instead of the sack. "Here you are."

Cheetah blew out her breath in a short, explosive way and started to turn. But the drawn-up right leg seemed to shoot pain through her reddish-gold body, and the mare stopped. "It's all right," I said soothingly. "It's OK."

Her huge brown eyes wide and alert, Cheetah swung her head back toward me. Carefully, she extended her muzzle toward my outstretched hand.

I held my breath.

In a long, agonizing moment, her lips touched the oats. This time, she did not turn away.

Cautiously I moved my left hand up to join the right from which she was eating. I paused, hardly able to breath. Then, very slowly, I moved my free hand to her nose. She smelled it noisily but did not jerk away.

In a moment, I was lightly stroking Cheetah's nose. In a few more moments, I was touching her neck. It was soft as the finest velvet, and was everything I'd thought it would be.

"Well, would you look at that!" The soft, awe-stricken words behind me caused Cheetah to throw her head up in fright. But she did not run. Instead, she stood trembling, facing the clearing.

"You did it!" Arlene's whispered words were filled with emotion. "You did it, Karen. You did it!"

"Yes," I replied. "At last Cheetah understands me and has come to me."

"How on earth did you do it?" she said.

"With oats," I said, "and love."

Cheetah began to lower her head toward my hand.

"Love," Arlene mused. "Love, the miracle-maker."

"Better not come any closer just yet," I cautioned. "She's eating out of my hand but her eyes are on you. She's coiled up tighter than a rattler. If she runs, she'll start to bleed again."

"I'm in no hurry," Arlene chuckled. "I'm enjoying the sight enough to stand here the rest of the day."

"That was a mighty brave thing you did a while ago," I said. "And foolish. That sow might have killed you."

"It was foolish, all right. Now that I think about it, I'm scared to death. But at the time, it seemed the only thing to do. Oh, by the way, the sow got tired of waiting for me to come down out of that second bunch of vines I climbed, so she took her litter and went off. But not before I worried myself sick over what you had found here."

"You love Cheetah too, don't you, Arlene?" My back was still toward her.

"Nipper I loved," she answered brightly. "No other horse could take his place. But Cheetah's got the best chance for second place, I guess."

I gave Cheetah the last of the oats. "Arlene, I'm glad you're my friend."

"It's nothing," she said seriously, then immediately

said in a light, teasing tone: "except downright dangerous, frustrating, and full of surprises."

"Cheetah and I think you're pretty wonderful," I replied.

"You speaking for the horse? She didn't say much yet."

"Honestly," I said, "I'll never forget what you did as
long as I live."

Arlene's reply was serious. "Me either—watching a
wild, untamed horse respond to your love."

"It took a long time," I admitted, "but Cheetah finally
realized I wouldn't hurt her."

The oats were gone. I let Cheetah sniff my hands. Then
I began to stroke her muzzle and neck. She stood on three
legs, still tensed, but not as tense as before. "Oh, Arlene,
how I longed for Cheetah to know how much I loved
her! How I wanted to share that love and have her
love me!"

Arlene chuckled. "Well, she does now! Just look at
her!"

"Nothing like it," I said happily, patting Cheetah's
neck.

"Well, now, that's a matter of opinion," Arlene said.

"What could be greater?" I asked happily.

"The love of—well, I wish your grandfather were here.
I get all tongue-tied, but he can say things—"

"A little bluntly," I finished, "but he says things. I'm
glad he's doing better." Then I started to cry again.

"Hey!" I heard Arlene move toward us and Cheetah
stepped back. "What's the matter?" Arlene demanded.

"I was just thinking," I blubbered.

"Thinking of what?"

"Grandad. What he thought. Oh, Arlene! I've been so
selfish!"

"All of us are, Karen. Don't take it so hard."

Cheetah pushed her muzzle against my hand to pet her. I began to do so, automatically, my mind on other things. "You know what Grandad would say, Arlene?"

She sounded puzzled. "No, what?"

"I'm sure he would say something about what was to be learned from all this. From this experience."

"I don't follow you."

I patted the mare absently. What should have been the greatest thrill of the summer was nothing. Ashes! Yes, I loved Cheetah and was glad she came around, but—

"What I'm saying," I said to Arlene, "is that I've made a couple of decisions in the last few hours."

"What kind of decisions?"

I blinked back tears. "Well, one came as a realization, I guess. The way I reached out to Cheetah with all my love is the way Christ has been reaching out to me."

Arlene was still standing behind me.

I continued, "Christ loves us—me, all of us—even though we're wild and, well, bad or sinful. Like I loved Cheetah in spite of her wildness."

"What're you saying, Karen?"

"That I want to become a Christian—a genuine, born-again Christian. Will you help me?"

"Of course!" I heard Arlene start toward me. The mare threw up her head in sudden fright. She whinnied and rolled her eyes. Arlene stopped.

"You'd better stay there," I cautioned, turning toward her, "at least till Cheetah gets used to you."

"I think you're right. Well, Karen, the first thing you need to know to accept Christ is that God loves you and you know that already."

"I sure do," I said.

"Secondly, you know that we're all sinners, and sin is anything that keeps us apart from God. And you know that Jesus' death is God's one way to pay for our sins, don't you?" Arlene asked.

I nodded.

"Then all you need to do now is tell God how you feel. Ask His forgiveness. Invite Christ into your life—to come in and to take control of it. Can you pray for that, Karen?"

I bowed my head. "Lord, I'm sorry for my sins. Forgive me. I accept Your Son Jesus as the sacrifice for my sins. I want Him to take charge of my life. Please—take my will and replace it with Yours. I ask this in Jesus' name. Amen."

"Amen!" Arlene repeated. Her eyes were sparkling with tears when I looked up. But her face was radiant. "Karen, the Bible says God won't turn anyone away who comes to Him," she added.

I felt doubtful. "I don't feel any different."

Arlene smiled broadly. "I don't remember when I was born into this world, and I'll bet you don't either. But the important thing is that you were—and, in this case, you are born-again. You should grow from now on."

"Well," I said a little uncertainly, patting Cheetah's sleek neck again, "I'd be happier if I felt something— some change."

"Faith counts, not feelings. Take it from someone who's been there. Feelings aren't necessary. You're a Christian now, Karen!"

I blinked tears from my eyelashes. "I wish Grandad were here."

"You can tell him as soon as possible. He'll be glad, I know."

"Yes," I agreed, "he will. Very glad. It means so much

to him to have people turn to Christ. Not just me, but people he meets, like Ted."

"Ted may be hard to reach," Arlene said.

"But if God can reach me, and I could reach Cheetah—with love—then Ted can be reached too. I've been wrong to treat him the way I have. I'd like to make it up to him. If I can talk to him about Christ, he'll know I'm really sorry."

"I'll help you," Arlene volunteered. "And speaking of helping, I wonder if Cheetah will let us treat that leg? She doesn't seem in too great pain, the way she keeps standing on three legs instead of lying down, but still—"

"I'd better try to look at that leg," I agreed.

"She might kick you."

"I don't think so. I'll go slowly. Besides, I've been thinking: she was not only hungry, she was hurting. And she's probably very tired. So accepting me just now was just a combination of a lot of things—love, need—"

Cheetah's ears went up. She tensed, her head high.

"Someone's coming," I said, glancing up the river the way Cheetah was looking.

"Probably Ted—out looking for us. I'd better go meet him so he doesn't scare Cheetah."

"Good idea! But do look out for those pigs! And ask him if he could cut a bunch of willows and make a corral here. Cheetah's not going anywhere on her own power until that leg is healed. We can't get a trailer down here through the brush. But we can get a vet. If we can close up the opening in the bushes here—"

"Great idea! The river will stop her from behind, and those berry bushes on the sides. Sure, it can be done!"

"I just hope she gets well fast. It would be terrible if she got a bad infection, or lockjaw—"

"She'll be just fine!" Arlene said emphatically. "After all, she's got someone to love her."

"You love her too, don't you, Arlene?"

"Almost as much as I loved Nipper." Arlene turned away. I could hear Ted whistling.

"Wait," I called.

"I was just going to meet Ted."

"He's still some distance away. But before he gets here, there's something I want to say to you."

"Oh, yes—I almost forgot. You said something about two decisions. What was the other?"

"Arlene," I said very slowly, "Cheetah—well—I've made up my mind."

"Made up your mind to what?"

I stroked the mare's neck. "Arlene, I want you to have Cheetah. I'm giving her to you."

CHAPTER 13

After the Darkness

ARLENE'S mouth dropped open.

"I mean it," I assured her. "I'm giving Cheetah to you."

Arlene managed to gasp, "But why?"

"Because she means too much to me. I've let my love for her push everybody and everything into second place —even God."

"Oh, it's not that serious, Karen!"

"Yes, it is. I want you to have her."

"Bu—but you're everything to Cheetah!"

"She's over the hump now. She knows you. She'll soon love you too."

Arlene shook her head. "I don't know, Karen."

"Don't you want her?" I asked.

"That's a silly question!"

"Then it's all settled. I'm giving her to you."

"Well, I really don't know—" She hesitated.

"Is it because she's cut up?" I demanded.

"You know better than that!" Arlene said.

"Then there's no need talking anymore about it. Cheetah is yours," I told her. I turned my back on Arlene again so she couldn't see my face. I reached up and patted the blaze on Cheetah's forehead. "You'd better go meet Ted," I said.

When Arlene and Ted approached a few minutes later, I had control of my emotions. I turned toward them, hoping my face wasn't red from crying. Cheetah trembled under my hand as Ted stopped outside the natural pen.

"What's this I hear about you giving the mare to Arlene?" he demanded.

"It's true," I said.

"You want my opinion?" Ted asked.

I managed to smile. "No, Ted, not really."

"I think you're out of your head," Ted said.

"Maybe so. But that's the way I see it."

"Nutty as a Christmas fruitcake," Ted insisted.

I kept the smile but didn't answer him.

Ted turned to Arlene. "Hey, what's wrong with her? She didn't bite my head off!"

"Aw, Ted," Arlene said, "leave her alone. She's just become a Christian."

"Is that why she's giving her horse away? If so, I don't want any part of that kind of religion!"

"Becoming a Christian isn't the reason I gave Cheetah to Arlene," I explained. "But there is a sort of tie-in."

"Well," Ted said, "you'd better explain it to me before I call the men with the butterfly nets to take you away."

"If you'll be serious, Ted," I told him, "I'll explain."

"I'd feel better if you fought with me like always," he said with a plaintive note in his voice. He obviously didn't know what to think of me in this new role.

"And that's another thing," I said to him. "I've been rude and unfair to you. I'm sorry, Ted. And do you know what the first commandment is?"

Ted almost seemed embarrassed at my apology but he said, "Sure. Something about not stealing; or is it about not killing?"

I shook my head. "The first commandment has to do with priorities—what God considers first and most important. He said, 'Thou shalt have none other gods before Me.'"

"So?" Ted asked.

"So," I shrugged, "I was putting Cheetah first in my life. Not worshiping her, of course, but putting her first; putting her between God and me. I loved her more than anybody, and that's not right."

"Even so, that's no reason to give her away," Ted said.

"It's my way of handling the problem, Ted," I said.

"I think you're still mixed up," he told me, soberly. "I see you standing there petting a horse that was wild as a mountain goat, and the only thing that influenced her was you."

"Her love," Arlene explained.

Ted shrugged. "OK, her love. Now," he turned to me, "you're going to take that love away from her so that you can love God. It just doesn't make sense to me."

"Arlene and Cheetah will love each other," I said calmly. "Now I don't want to talk about it anymore. Tell me, what do you think of the idea of fixing up a temporary corral here?"

Ted glanced around. "No trouble. Arlene explained your idea. All I need is some tools."

"Then could you get them and begin work?" I asked. "It'll be sundown before you can possibly finish."

Ted grinned. "Daylight saving time in the summer means light until about 8:30. I'll have your—uh—Arlene's horse safely penned in before then."

I stayed with Cheetah through the pounding and digging noises. I didn't get a real good look at the hurt leg, but Cheetah let me get close enough to see that it wasn't too serious. Ted brought hay for the mare when he returned with his tools, so Cheetah was all set for the night when we finally left her. I didn't look back as I walked away. Cheetah nickered softly after me, but I resisted the temptation to look.

Mom greeted me at the door. "You're just in time! Your father called from the next town. He said the bus would be pulling into Oakvalley by the time I can drive in to meet him. He wanted you to come too, Karen."

"It'll be good to see him," I said. "Have you heard about Grandad?"

"I had just phoned the hospital before your father called. The doctor said he's doing very well."

"I'd like to talk to him, Mom."

"The hospital won't let you in for a while, dear." Mom looked curiously at me. "Why is it so important that you talk to him?"

"I've got a couple things to tell him."

"Tell me while we drive. But first, you'd better take a second to clean up. You're a mess from all that river brush."

We were rolling smoothly through the darkness in Mom's car when I told her what I'd wanted to speak to Grandad about. "Mom," I began, staring ahead at the headlights on the country road, "I accepted Christ this afternoon."

"You did?" Mom cried. She reached over with her right arm and hugged me to her. "When? Where?"

I told her.

"I'm so delighted," Mom said. "And your grandfather will be especially happy."

I told Mom about Cheetah coming up to me, and how I petted her.

"That's remarkable," Mom said. "And a good thing too, with your father coming home. You know how firm he can be. He wouldn't have let you keep a wild horse."

"It's all right, Mom," I said quietly. "I gave Cheetah to Arlene."

Mom glanced at me in the car's half-light. "Wasn't that a little drastic, dear?"

"I don't think so. Besides, you've been wanting me to get rid of her, and now, well, everything's fine."

Mom asked slowly, "Did you give up the mare because of my objections or fear your father might make you get rid of her?"

"I thought of all those things," I confessed, "but the real reason I gave Cheetah away was to prevent her from coming between me and God."

Mother was quiet for a while. Finally she said, "Do you really think that was necessary, Karen?"

"Mom, I've been so confused. It seemed like the right thing to do."

"Well, you know what your problem is now. I would think that if you put God first, Karen, then you could still love Cheetah—but just make sure you keep her in her place. It's a matter of priorities. We all love others. I love you, your father, grandfather, brothers, and sisters. But I can't give any of you away, can I?"

"No, of course not. But Cheetah's different."

"Is she?" Mom asked. Then she went on, "Of course, there are some things people should give up to lead a good Christian life. But I don't think you needed to give up the mare."

I said nothing. I had a vaguely uneasy feeling. Had I gone too far? Had I? If living a Christian life was going to start off like this—

Mom seemed to know what I was thinking. She reached over and patted my knee. "God knows you've meant to please Him," she said. "Just remember, 'All things work together for good to them that love God.'"

I was still thinking about that when we pulled up in front of the bus depot. We checked at the counter and learned the bus was running a little late. It was a beautiful, warm summer night, so Mom and I stood outside on the curb. I looked up at the stars and wondered many things—

"Hey, Karen!" The voice jerked me back to the present.

Ted's pickup truck pulled up to the curb. Arlene jumped out and ran up to me. "I just had to find you!" she cried.

I felt a moment of fear. "Something happened to Cheetah?"

"No! Yes!" Arlene laughed.

"Well, make up your mind," I said, half seriously.

Ted got out of the truck and came around to stand with us. He spoke politely to Mom and then said, "You'd better tell her, Arlene."

"Tell me what?" I demanded.

Arlene took me by the shoulders and looked squarely into my face. The streetlight glinted in her bright eyes. "I don't know why I didn't think of it before—"

"Arlene!" I said with some exasperation.

"I've been thinking," Arlene said in a rush, "and I was wrong."

Mom seemed as perplexed as I was. "What are you talking about, Arlene?"

Ted said, "Remember why Cheetah wanted to get out?"

Mom answered for me. "The mare got out because Karen's grandfather had a heart attack, and she rushed off without properly bolting the horse corral gate."

Arlene was fairly dancing on the curb with excitement. "That's only part of it! We all knew Cheetah had been restless, but none of us realized why." Arlene looked at me triumphantly. "Cheetah wanted a mate!"

Ted agreed. "That's why she got out and jumped that barbed wire fence—so she could find Sinbad."

"And that means—" Arlene was dancing up and down. "That means Cheetah will probably have a colt. Right?"

Mom and I looked at each other. "I hadn't thought of it, but I guess that's right," I agreed.

Arlene was almost pulling me off my feet, she was so excited. "That's what I thought! You hadn't expected that. So a colt would be a sort of bonus, wouldn't it?"

"I guess you could say that. Why?"

"Well, I've got an idea!"

Mother sputtered, "Arlene, please get to the point!"

"OK," Arlene agreed, forcing herself to be calm, "Ted's father usually gets a fee for grade mares standing to Sinbad, and I'll gladly pay that fee if—"

"If what, Arlene?" I asked.

"If I can have Cheetah's colt!"

I felt let down. "Cheetah is already yours, Arlene, so of course the foal would be yours too."

Arlene started dancing again. "That's what I've been trying to say! I'd rather have the colt than Cheetah!"

I guess my mouth dropped open.

"Well," Arlene demanded excitedly, "how about it? You keep Cheetah and give me her colt! OK?"

It took me a moment to fully understand what she was saying. I looked up at the sky, said softly, "Thanks, Lord!" Then I grabbed Arlene in a wild dance.

I also let out a yell which Grandpa later insisted he heard at the nearby hospital. In fact, over a year and a half later, he was still teasing me about it as I rode Cheetah around the ranch.

"They were ready to evacuate the hospital," Grandpa said from where he sat under the shade of a chinaberry tree. "But I told them it was just my granddaughter celebrating with the Lord's own joy."

I reined Cheetah around and grinned down at Grandpa. "You shouldn't tell such whoppers," I scolded. "Remember what you used to tell me about the tongue keeping people out of heaven, same's murder!"

"Nothing's going to keep me out of heaven," Grandpa said.

Cheetah's ears swiveled toward the road and she whinnied. Both Grandpa and I spun around to see what had attracted the mare's attention.

Arlene was just entering the gate. She was leading a beautiful colt by a training halter. The colt was a mixture of reddish-gold and chocolate with glistening highlights. It had Sinbad's dish-faced Arabian head and Cheetah's intelligent, loving eyes. Ted was riding Sinbad a few paces behind them.

"Grandpa," I said softly, "nothing's going to keep me out of heaven either."

Then I loosened the reins and let Cheetah trot proudly toward the group at the gate.